Just Gaming

Theory and History of Literature
Edited by Wlad Godzich and Jochen Schulte-Sasse

Volume 1.   Tzvetan Todorov *Introduction to Poetics*

Volume 2.   Hans Robert Jauss *Toward an Aesthetic of Reception*

Volume 3.   Hans Robert Jauss
Aesthetic Experience and Literary Hermeneutics

Volume 4.   Peter Burger *Theory of the Avant-Garde*

Volume 5.   Vladimir Propp *Theory and History of Folklore*

Volume 6.   Edited by Jonathan Arac, Wlad Godzich,
and Wallace Martin
The Yale Critics: Deconstruction in America

Volume 7.   Paul de Man *Blindness and Insight:*
Essays in the Rhetoric of Contemporary Criticism
2nd ed., rev.

Volume 8.   Mikhail Bakhtin *Problems of Dostoevsky's Poetics*

Volume 9.   Erich Auerbach
Scenes from the Drama of European Literature

Volume 10. Jean-François Lyotard
The Postmodern Condition: A Report on Knowledge

Volume 11. Edited by John Fekete *The Structural Allegory:*
Reconstructive Encounters with the New French Thought

Volume 12. Ross Chambers *Story and Situation: Narrative Seduction and*
the Power of Fiction

Volume 13. Tzvetan Todorov *Mikhail Bakhtin: The Dialogical Principle*

Volume 14. Georges Bataille *Visions of Excess: Selected Writings,*
1927-1939

Volume 15. Peter Szondi *On Textual Understanding and Other Essays*

Volume 16. Jacques Attali *Noise*

Volume 17. Michel de Certeau *Heterologies*

Volume 18. Thomas G. Pavel *The Poetics of Plot:*
The Case of English Renaissance Drama

Volume 19. Jay Caplan *Framed Narratives:*
Diderot's Genealogy of the Beholder

Volume 20. Jean-François Lyotard and Jean-Loup Thébaud
Just Gaming

Just Gaming

Jean-François Lyotard and Jean-Loup Thébaud

Translated by Wlad Godzich

Afterword by Samuel Weber

Translated by Brian Massumi

Theory and History of Literature, Volume 20

 University of Minnesota Press, Minneapolis

The University of Minnesota Press gratefully acknowledges
translation assistance provided for this book by the
French Ministry of Culture.

English translation and Introduction copyright 1985 by the University of Minnesota
Originally published in France as *Au Juste*
Copyright Christian Bourgois, editeur, 1979

Fifth Printing, 1999

Published by the University of Minnesota Press,
111 Third Avenue South, Suite 290,
Minneapolis, MN 55401-2520
Printed in the United States of America
http://www.upress.umn.edu
Library of Congress Cataloging in Publication Data

Lyotard, Jean-Francois.
  Just Gaming.
  (Theory and History of Literature; v. 20)
  Translation of: Au Juste.
  Includes index.
  1. Languages—Philosophy.   2. Philosophical recreations.
I. Thébaud, Jean-Loup.   II. Title.   III. Series.
P106.L9313   1985   793.73   85-1109
ISBN 0-8166-1281-1
ISBN 0-8166-1277-3 (pbk.)

The University of Minnesota
is an equal-opportunity
educator and employer.

Contents

First Day   The Impossible Consensus   3

Second Day   The Three Pragmatic Positions   19

Third Day   A General Literature   44

Fourth Day   A Casuistry of the Imagination   60

Fifth Day   A Politics of Judgment   73

Sixth Day   The Faculty of Political Ideas   84

Seventh Day Majority Does Not Mean Great Number
                        But Great Fear   93

Afterword   Literature — Just Making It
                        by Samuel Weber   101

Index   123

Just Gaming

The rule of the undetermined
is itself undetermined.

Nicomachean Ethics **1137b29-30**

First Day
The Impossible Consensus

JFL: You are saying about my *L'Économie libidinale* that its mode of writing is such as to make it a take-it-or-leave-it proposition. I will answer: You take it or leave it, but if you leave it, it means that it has produced no effects.

JLT: I was saying that the form of writing did not allow for any negotiating.

JFL: I wonder if any book is ever negotiable, in any case. I think books produce effects. Those that pretend to negotiate are somewhat naive.

JLT: If both parties, author and reader, are neutralized, then one can say: Let's talk. But your entire book has been written in such a way as to exclude this possibility. This is why I have been thinking that it will be very difficult to have a conversation with the author of that book.

JFL: Yes. But it does not mean that discussion is impossible. It does mean that a certain kind of discussion is indeed difficult. I don't say impossible because it is not true that the theoretical is altogether absent from it. Rather, it is quite a bit distorted. It has been infiltrated by something else. It is not a theoretical discourse in the strict sense of the term, and I suppose it must have given fits of laughter to the two or three logicians who have taken a peak at the book. Nonetheless, one of the possible effects of this book is for people to want to discuss some of the things that are to be found in it with the one who wrote them. And, in point of fact, that has happened.

A little more on this subject before it bores us utterly. For me, it is actually a problem. Here is a book the writing of which is meant to stay clear from a certain kind of commentary, to be sure, and therefore, insofar as it does not lend itself to dialogue, it perpetrates a kind of violence. Perhaps one should go even further: It does not lend itself to dialectics in Aristotle's sense of the term, that is, it does not lend itself to a discussion bearing on opinions, because, to some extent, it is not so much the opinions to be found in the book that stand in the way of discussion. This book has been written in scandalous fashion. What is scandalous about it is that it is all rhetoric; it works entirely at the level of persuasion, the old *Peithô*, and even if the turns it uses were not controlled (for the most part, they were not), the "calculated" (but uncontrolled) effect was certainly not that of a pedagogy, nor that of a dialectic; it was much more poetic, more literary, but in a somewhat odd sense of the term. It is a book that belongs more to the verbal arts than to philosophical writing, including dialectics, I would reiterate. In that sense, I understand what you mean, but the question that I ask myself with respect to your attitude is why you have picked this reserve, this holding back of mine, that says: This is a book that aims to produce effects upon the reader, and its author does not ask that these effects be sent back to him in the forms of questions.

This kind of writing is generally taken to be that of the rhetorician and of the persuader, that is, of the maker of simulacra, of the sly one, the one who deceives. To me, it is the opposite. That is, in ancient thought, since Platonism let us say, the rhetorician, the orator, the poet, etc., is precisely the one who seeks to produce effects upon the other, effects that the other does not control. But if you take dialogic discourse, as Plato presents it, it is a discourse in which each of the participants is, in principle, trying to produce statements such that the effects of these statements can be sent back to their author so that he may say: This is true, this is not true, and so on. In other words, so that he can control, or contribute to the control of, these effects. In the writing of the *L'Économie libidinale*, there is a reversal with respect to this tradition: the regulating of dialogic discourse, even of dialectical discourse in the Platonic sense, seemed to me to be associated with power, since ultimately it aims at controlling the effects of the statements exchanged by the partners of the dialogue; I was trying, on the contrary, to limit myself to the delivery of a mass of statements barely controlled in themselves, and, insofar as the relation to the addressee is concerned, they were drawn up more in the spirit of the bottle tossed into the ocean than in that of a return of the effects of the statements to their author. Without knowing it, I was experimenting also with a pragmatics that, for some Sophists, is a decisive aspect of the poetic: It is true that the poet is not concerned, after his statements are made, to enter into a dialogue with his readers in order to establish whether or not they understood him.

JLT: With this difference though: there is, in your book, a great violence.

JFL: But no more than in poetic or literary writing. . . .

JLT: What is different is that there is here a constraint of opinion.

JFL: I believe that there is indeed a constraint. The difference, a surface one in any case (I am not sure that it is real) with poetic or literary writing is that, in principle, the book remains a theoretical book; the background of the book is, in any case, theoretical; it puts forward certain theses, and insofar as these theses are advanced not in order to convince or to refute but to persuade—let us say, to take hold of or to let go—then indeed the distance between the *lexis*, that is, the mode of presentation, on the one hand, and the *logos*, that is, the content, on the other, this distance perpetrates violence: these theses are not up for discussion. But actually they can be discussed. I mean that it is also possible to read the book skipping over all the rhetorical machinery, whether spontaneous or not, and to take only the theses, and perhaps one can realize then that the book is completely inconsistent from this point of view. Why not? It presupposes that the reader does not allow himself or herself to be intimidated, if I may say so.

JLT: It presupposes that you are willing to discuss the theses, with the presupposition that is attached to any thesis, namely, that it is universalizable and that anyone can claim it as his or her own.

JFL: That is what I meant. The difference between what I write and poetry and literature is that, in principle, what I write is not fiction. But I do wonder more and more: Is there a real difference between a theory and a fiction? After all, don't we have the right to present theoretical statements under the form of fictions, in the form of fictions? Not *under* the form, but *in* the form.

JLT: That makes a conversation more and more impossible.

JFL: But no more impossible than a conversation with a [fiction] writer.

JLT: Yes, but with a writer, the "form" of the conversation is entirely different.

JFL: Which means that it is not really a matter of arriving at the truth of the content of the theses of the book, but rather a question of coming to grips with the new effects produced by the new situation of a joint discussion. And there will be no attempt then, in the book we are trying to produce now, to tell the truth of *L'Économie libidinale* and the other books; it will be rather an attempt to produce a new book. The effects that had been produced upon us will be constitutive elements of the new book (the book of our conversations), and the latter will not be the clarification, the correct version, of the previous ones, but one of their effects upon two addressees, you and me, who are in no way privileged. . . .

JLT: You do have some privileges that I don't in this though.*

JFL: Because you suppose a mastery of the author in relation to the reader. But what actually obtains in the relation constituted by these conversations? I have written books that have been sent off like bottles to the sea, and you, you have read them; you are a reader, a reader who asks questions, and not only who asks questions but who proposes interpretations of the matters read. You are a reader who starts to talk. Now, a reader is an addressee of written messages. A reader who starts to talk is something else: someone who takes the position of a sender of new messages. Even if the message is a question; even if the message awaits an answer. In this way, there is in our present game a certain reversal of roles, since I am the one who tries to listen to your questions and to speak in turn from them. Insofar as what I wrote raised questions for you, you ask questions that in turn will raise questions for me: there is a permutation, an exchange of roles, in the very production of this book. It is not, and cannot be, a book about my previous books, since, in it, I am not he who wrote these books but he who listens to the one who has read them, namely you. Here is a book of "mine" that I will not have written.

---

*It will have been noted [in the French text] that JLT uses the *vous* form to JFL while JFL uses the *tu* to JLT. This inequality in the use of the forms of address may be taken as the mark of a relation of superiority. Something else is actually at play here. Two types of relation are partially covered, and uncovered, by this asymmetry. The use of the *tu* form connotes also political comradeship (which was not direct in this instance). But then, it will be said, why is it not reciprocated? Because the comradeship was sufficiently distant not to be able to efface the reserve one feels towards the stranger. The distribution of pronouns as it obtains here is governed as well by the custom on relations between an older and a younger person, for example. In any case, its opposite would not be either the use of the mutual *tu* or of the mutual *vous*: the good reversibility is the one that does not mask the irreversibility of relations.

JLT: All these permutations take place in a common space that was opened by you. These questions are going to be mostly requests for further clarification, requests for glosses.

JFL: That remains to be seen. It is likely that in the questions that you will ask there will be things I have not thought of, and that this will force me to change considerably some of my positions. To that extent, this is going to be an experience quite different from that of writing, for me. And I owe it to you. Which proves once more that the problem is not one of mastery, since, here, I am "un-mastered." I therefore think that these permutations are far from being of little import, at least not for me. Anyway, does a "request for clarification" mean anything but an invitation to the speaker to change problematics? So that the result is not a clarification but an obscurity. And the obscurity of the clarification testifies to the fact that the speaker is dispossessed of his mastery.

JLT: It could also be said, quite to the contrary, that he redoubles it, that it is an opportunity to be masterful in another way.

JFL: No. Because when one is subjected to questioning in a conversation, one is placed on a ground where one is not at all assured of one's mastery, where one can be completely new, innocent, even stupid.

JLT: I grant you that there could be at times surprise effects.

JFL: Much more than that. And something else also.

JLT: But what is specific to these colloquies is that it is incumbent upon you, from the position of mastery that is yours, to constantly reoccupy the ground and to reorder the discourse.

JFL: That depends on the direction of the answers. One can try to give answers by getting back from the externality, the forcignness, of the ground to which one has been led, to the familiarity of known ground, by showing that this is but another way of speaking, and that it is really the same thing. On the other hand, one can answer by trying to change, that is, by saying: Yes, this is a question I had not thought of, and here is what I feel like saying about that, without at all caring whether or not it is coherent or consistent with something that I have already written.

At such a moment, one gives up one's mastery and one speaks in undigested fashion. In these pragmatic conditions, I don't see at all what privileges I could have. I don't have any. I am like someone who is asked a sudden question on topics he is not at all familiar with and in places where he holds no advantage. It is not merely a matter of surprise; it is a difference of language game.

JLT: I am nonetheless struck by the fact that the style of these conversations will not resemble at all that of most of your books.

JFL: Generally speaking, writing is irresponsible, in the strict sense of the term, because it does not come in response to a question. It proceeds of its own pace. Montaigne is the absolute model here. Writing marches to its own beat and it has no debts. Whereas in the style of the conversations we are having, I feel indebted in relation to the questions you are asking of me. The result is that what I say is always finalized by a question.

JLT: Yes. I believe that in writing there is a surfeit of artifices that, contrarily to what one may think, makes for more vivaciousness than is possible in speech. The latter may appear vivacious at first but actually is not that much.

JFL: Yes, I agree wholeheartedly. Orality is not vivaciousness. This is the danger of this oral work.

JLT: This is a delusion common to this type of book, I think.

JFL: Yes, if it is a genre that aims at vivaciousness. But if it aims at something else, if it aims at accessibility, that is, if it demands of the writer of books that she get out of the solitude and irresponsibility in which she writes and that she put herself in a position of partnership in which she asks questions and gives replies, in other words, that she takes a position analogous to yours right now, then it is true that this is a worthwhile experiment. If it were up to me alone, I would never do it.

JLT: We are reaching the paradox that the existence of the reader is a cross for the author.

JFL: Yes, I believe that one cannot write, in the broad sense of the term, with the reader, especially when one is just writing, when writing is its own main objective. One writes only in the reader's absence. I mean not only in the physical absence of a reader; there must be a kind of absence of readers to write the way some of us wish to write. The reader's solicitation, or what one imagines it to be, must be suspended and, in a way, one must have no interest in it. Then one can speed along and use the artifices, the ruses, you were speaking of.

JLT: But the dedications? The acknowledgments of indebtedness?

JFL: I don't think that it is true that one writes for someone. After the fact, one can say: this is a book for this type of or that type of person or persons. Or one can do as Butor does and dedicate one book to the people in the provinces and another to the Indians. But this is a bestowal, an act of giving, that is part of the book; it is not a destination of the writing. I believe that it is important that there be no addressee. When you cast bottles to the waves, you don't know to whom they are going, and that is all to the good. That must be part of modernity, I think.

JLT: What do you mean by modernity?

JFL: When someone like Corneille does an analysis of his tragedies, these analyses are intended for a public, for a set of readers, for a definite cultural group. He justifies, he defends, what he has done in the name of a system of values that are the values held by this public, which happens to be his public. Actually this is what I would call classicism: a situation in which an author can write while putting himself at the same time in the position of a reader, being able to substitute himself for his own reader, and to judge and sort out what he has accomplished from the point of view of the reader that he also is. The writer knows the solicitation that is addressed to him; he shares it in his capacity as reader; he answers it in his capacity as writer. Whereas in what we call modernity, he no longer knows for whom he writes, since there no longer is any taste; there no longer is any internalized system of rules that would permit a sorting out, the dropping of some things and the introduction of some others, all of this before the fact, in the act of writing. We are without interlocutors. The book takes off in networks of distribution that are not at all networks of reception. They are economic networks, sales networks. And as to what may happen to the book, what its actual reception may be, no one really knows.

If there is in the framework of this modernity something that would be equivalent to classicism, it is fashion. The criteria for the reception of books are not held to be well-grounded values in themselves, but rather to be arbitrary systems of selection with a limited life expectancy. This expectation produces a pressure upon the person writing; it prescribes a number of connotations by means of which the public recognizes what it expects and selects the writers that actually comply with the expectations. But, in contradistinction to classicism, regulation through fashion is half-cynical, half-shameful. Actually, it is subject to a situation that is very little classical: writing as research. The instability of criteria, even in fashions, comes from this experimental situation. It also makes for the fact that today the majority of people who write interesting things, write without knowing to whom they are speaking. That is part of the workings of this society, and it is very good. There is no need to cry about it.

Let us look at this from another perspective. I am thinking of the strictures addressed to the artistic vanguard: "You are doing things that nobody can understand, and you are wrong." It is the old indictment drawn up against the Russian vanguard in the years 1918-25: The drama of Lunacharsky or that of Maiakovsky, Lenin's thundering pronouncements. All of that is part of the same problem: the artistic vanguard knows that it has no readers, no viewers, and no listeners. If, on the other hand, it is saddled with the image of a reader, viewer, or listener, if, in other words, the contour of an addressee is imposed upon it, and this contour filters out the experiments in sound, form, literature, and even theory, that the vanguard is allowed to make, then it will not be able to do anything. There is an important issue here: the problem is not only political, in the usual and simple sense of the term, but it is a problem of how one views history and society. When one says: There are no readers for the people who write, no viewers for those who paint, no listeners for those who compose, it means that there is no subject of history. One cannot work telling oneself that, yes, there are values that arranged in a specific way form a subject. This is the subject to whom I speak: I communicate what I have to say in its name. To presuppose such an addressee or tutor, is to admit that all the actions that form history, including those of the works in question, find their ultimate meaning in the accomplishments of a universal subject. It is the idea of such a subject that modern artists refuse.

What is at stake in artistic language today is experimentation. And to experiment means, in a way, to be alone, to be celibate. But, on the other hand, it also means that if the artifact produced is really strong, it will wind up producing its own readers, its own viewers, its own listeners. In other words, the experimental work will have as one of its effects the constitution of a pragmatic situation that did not exist before. It is the message itself, by its form, that will elicit both the one who receives it and the one who sends it. They are able then to communicate with each other. And, as you know, sometimes this takes centuries, sometimes twenty years, sometimes three, and there are times when it happens right away. I don't believe that there are any rules in these matters. But what is beyond doubt is the fact that if the work is strong (and we don't really know what we are saying by this) it will produce people to whom it is destined. It will elicit its own addressees. These are things that Barthes had seen. I think that such is modernity. It does not lend itself at all to the legitimation of the jeremiads of the misunderstood artist or of the haughtiness of the genius ahead of his time. Communication simply does not obtain because the value system is not sufficiently stable for a work to be able to find its appointed place and to be assured of a hearing.

JLT: Two questions then: Is romanticism part of modernity? What is meant exactly when one speaks of the "modern" writer? Is the modernity of the modern writer something else than the fact of writing in a modern society?

JFL: Yes and no. To begin with the first point, with romanticism, it is difficult to answer; the word has taken on such a broad extension.

JLT: An approximation may do, as it did in the case of classicism.

JFL: For classicism, it is relatively easier, and actually the approximation is sufficiently rigorous.

JLT: Yes, there are rules and a public.

JFL: Let us take up the matter of "pleasing." What does "to please" mean? It means that there are judgments of taste, and that these judgments are universal. In other words, things are there; they are in place. Obviously romanticism presents itself as something modern with respect to classicism. But it has tried to reproduce a classical schema, at least insofar as the issue of the addressee that is of interest to us is concerned. It has tried to reconstruct a general configuration of the reader, a kind of universality, by drawing upon popular tradition. What was new about it was the appearance of the people as a potential public. Stable judgments of taste, already in place in the popular tradition, can then be supposed, and new works can be created with these judgments as models.

JLT: Classical theater rested upon aristocratic society. There was then a specified audience, a definite public. The rules that had to be observed in order to stage a work that would please the court, were known. You are saying that, with romanticism, the people comes forth in turn as the bearer of judgments of taste?

JFL: I would like to interrupt us here a little. What was really modern is what happened between the two, between classicism and romanticism, not the *Aufklärung* [Enlightenment] itself as such, because it remains universalist, but within that movement, the individuals who did not have such a simple idea of what humanity, and therefore the eventual public for the works, could be. I am thinking of someone like Diderot, who knows very well that the traditional, learned court public is about to disappear, but he does not think that another public of equally strong constitution is about to manifest itself; nor does he think that the people can be such a public. And so he finds himself in the in-between; he is modern. Not all of Diderot, but perhaps the Diderot of the *Salons*, and especially the Diderot of the *Neveu de Rameau* and of *Jacques le fataliste*. . . . Let us say the Diderot who begins to work with new literary operators that interest us today because they imply among other things, the evanescence of the addressee. One can find in his writings substitutions in the pragmatic system of the narration, permutations of the author with the narrator, of the narrattee with the speaker and with the one who is spoken of in the narrative, and so on, . . . The three narrative positions are in a state of permutation, not a continuous one to be sure, for that would be too simple, but a frequent and an aleatory one. So that we get something that is not unrelated to romantic irony, but is actually humor. I think that humor is an essential tone of modernity. It is also Mallarmé's humor.

JLT: So we would have romanticism bound up by the category of irony (which is what Hegel was saying). . . .

JFL: . . . that consists in going beyond the law of classicism in the matter of the reader, that is, the law of taste, by discovering a new reader above this law, in a beyond of taste. . . .

JLT: . . . who knows the law and parodies it. Whereas humor would be one of the characteristics of modernity.

JFL: Yes, it is characteristic of the experimenter, of any experimenter.

JLT: Then I would say that there are presently few works that are modern.

JFL: Why is that?

JLT: Simply because many of the so-called modern works of today have a public that is their own. A very simple instance: pop music is not modern; it is as classical as can be, because it is addressed to a certain audience, and it just is not true that it is not known whom it is addressed to. It is still a question of pleasing and affecting.

JFL: How are you taking the term "pop music?" Do you take it as a collective term encompassing all the variants within?

JLT: Yes.

JFL: That is a lot of variants.

JLT: The term says it well: "popular music," which means that its support and its addressee are indeed the people.

JFL: No, it means popular in the sense that in modernity there is no longer a people. Within pop music, there are elements that are popular in the romantic sense of the term. I am thinking of the re-discovery of popular musics that are not pop music but that can be very well integrated into pop music. There are many examples of this. These popular elements, in the romantic sense, refer back to ethnic traditions, both European and non-European ones. This type of search appears to carry out the same tasks as romanticism; I say "appears" because actually it does not. Because these popular musics are reintegrated into the enormous mass of pop music, as one of its variants, and since pop music itself is not ethnic music, it cannot really be considered popular music in the sense in which there would be a people that would be at once its audience, its performer, and its composer, having found within it its own canons. On the contrary, what strikes me about pop music, and it is particularly apparent in the United States, is that it is an immense, monstrous body that does no more than bring forth, year after year, new variants, new sound organizations, that previously were unheard. The variants may at times be quite far-reaching; they play upon the harmonic system, upon preferred melodic rhetorics, or upon the instrumental system used, etc. When these new arrangements are brought out, they have no audience. They will find one; they will be liked, although sometimes it does not work. Sometimes it does. One does not know at first, and the artist who sets out to do it has no idea whether it will work or not, especially since his or her work is experimental in nature. Pop music, in spite of its name, is not a music of the people, in the romantic sense of the term.

JLT: . . . to the precise extent that the people here is not the romantics' people.

JFL: It is indeed not the people of the romantics at all. It is a kind of ocean within which there will coalesce for a while an ear for hearing the music, bodies to dance to it, and voices to sing it. And then after a while, it will disappear to reappear later, but with another ear, another voice. . . . This immense kind of thing does not have its own stable sound-filtering system.

JLT: Let us return to what I was saying earlier. If I understand you correctly, it would seem that the essential feature of modernity is its untimeliness. It is in that spirit that I was saying that pop music is not modern. It is not untimely; it goes straight to the core of the social body as it exists today. The people is no longer what it once was; it is no longer an organic body as the people was for Michelet, and the music that is produced and corresponds to this body cannot have popular features in the sense of Grimm or of Dvořák. I come back to my previous remark: There is not much that is modern in modern authors. They are modern because everyone is. But they are not untimely; they are not modern in the sense that you mean.

JFL: Untimeliness can be defined in the strong sense, as in Nietzsche, but I think that Nietzsche's strong sense still belongs very much to romantic irony: it implies a position on the part of the author, his or her disagreement with the established public of contemporaries, the disavowal of her or his time. This is not all that Nietzsche meant, of course, but he does fall into a certain misprision here. Untimeliness is not therefore the sign of modernity in the sense we mean. It can be a romantic marker, and the romantic is not the modern. There is no nostalgia in the modern. It is threatened from another side: I think that it is very difficult to distinguish, when a modern work appears, between that by which it is truly modern, in the sense of experimental, and that by which it is merely innovative, that is, where it is but a way of repeating, without great difference, something that has already been done and that has worked. Innovation within fashion. I believe that these kinds of distinctions must be made one at a time, and without criteria.

JLT: Yes, but how do we do it, if there is no *sensus communis*?

JFL: There cannot be a *sensus communis*.

JLT: Yet we do make judgments; there must be a *sensus communis.*

JFL: No, we judge without criteria. We are in the position of Aristotle's prudent individual, who makes judgments about the just and the unjust without the least criterion.

JLT: Yet, you distinguish between experimental works and mere innovations.

JFL: Yes, I make such a distinction, and I believe that it is an understandable one, but I also believe that, when a new work appears, it is difficult to reach immediate aggreement on whether the work is a modern one in the sense that it tests hitherto untouched limits of sensibility or of culture, or whether it complements an already explored field.

JLT: Is it time that decides? I would not think so!

JFL: No, no! Neither time nor the concept. It is decided, that is all that can be said. We are dealing with judgments that are not regulated by categories. History itself provides no help in their formulation, at least not on the spot. For it to do so, one would have to presuppose that history proceeds by concepts, dialectically. Whereas it guides us only after the fact.

JLT: Don't you have the feeling that you are writing, book after book, a new *Critique of Judgment*?

JFL: I would not say so. I would not let myself say so. Anyway, what does a "new Critique of Judgment" mean?

JLT: In this instance, it means the working out of criteria that allows us to decide what is modern and what is not. Because you always do decide. I am thinking of your article on Louis Marin's *Critique du discours*.

JFL: Absolutely. But, to begin with, I may be wrong. Secondly, I may be the only one to hold a given opinion. Thirdly, I may change my mind about a judgment I have made. I mean that, in each instance, I have a feeling, that is all. It is a matter of feelings, however, in the sense that one can judge without concepts. Let me take the example of Marin, since you have brought it up: my feeling is that Pascal is modern precisely because he takes on the question of criteria of judgments. Marin comes at it from semiotics. Semiotics is nothing but criteria and relevant features for judging works: nothing less modern. In order to understand Pascal, Marin drops semiotics: he is modern. In the same way, I would say that a given ancient philosophy of language, such as that of Antisthenes, which attempts to escape predication and definition, is modern by this very token.

JLT: But what are you saying? I think, I find, I estimate, therefore I judge?

JFL: Absolutely. I judge. But if I am asked by what criteria do I judge, I will have no answer to give. Because if I did have criteria, if I had a possible answer to your question, it would mean that there is actually a possible consensus on these criteria between the readers and me; we would not be then in a situation of modernity, but in classicism. What I mean is that anytime that we lack criteria, we are in modernity, wherever we may be, whether it be at the time of Augustine, Aristotle, or Pascal. The date does not matter.

JLT: But in the preface to *Rudiments Païens* [*Pagan Rudiments*] you say that the instructions for the ideas advanced in that book will be forthcoming. That could lead one to think that you are working out "critical" concepts by which modernity is meant to be judged.

JFL: "Rudiments," as the little preamble you mentioned explains, are studies that are left undeveloped. The material itself is not refined; it is in the process of refining itself. It will be, I hope, the book

I am working on now. But that does not mean that the criteria absent from *Rudiments païens* will be found there. It means in fact the very opposite: there are still too many criteria in *Rudiments* and there will be far fewer in the "refined" book. But I wanted to add that when I speak of paganism, I am not using a concept. It is a name, neither better nor worse than others, for the denomination of a situation in which one judges without criteria. And one judges not only in matters of truth, but also in matters of beauty (of aesthetic efficacy) and in matters of justice, that is, of politics and ethics, and all without criteria. That's what I mean by paganism.

If one examines the actual state of affairs in the stories of Greek and Roman mythology, and especially if one pays attention to the words and the actions, one cannot fail to notice that there is no stable system to guide judgments. When we say: There is ruse, as Détienne and Vernant observe in their very impressive book, we mean that ruse is not just a technique or a device for the purpose of overcoming one's opponents; it is much more than that. Ruse is an activity bound up with the will to power, because the will to power, if the word is to have a meaning, is carried out without criteria. Ruse is used on grounds and in fields, in both the topological and in the chronological sense, precisely where there are no criteria. That's what I mean by "pagan." I believe that modernity is pagan.*

JLT: But you mean two things with "pagan." First, it is a word that denotes a specific system, that of modernity, and then, it is a prescription, since you enjoin whoever wants to write, to move in that direction, instead of going in the direction of Corneille or of Racine.

JFL: Oh, yes, absolutely. Just yesterday, someone asked me rather flippantly, "Well, why do you write?" that is, not: what are your reasons for writing? but, what system of justification do you give yourself? I answered without a second's hesitation that I have always

---

*JFL believes that he can dissipate today (October 1979) some of the confusion that prevails in this conversation on modernity by introducing a distinction between the modern and the postmodern within that which is confused here under the first term. The modern addressee would be the "people," an idea whose referent oscillates between the romantics' *Volk* and the *fin-de-siècle* bourgeoisie. Romanticism would be modern as would the project, even if it turns out to be impossible, of elaborating a taste, even a "bad" one, that permits an evaluation of works. Postmodern (or pagan) would be the condition of the literatures and arts that have no assigned addressee and no regulating ideal, yet in which value is regularly measured on the stick of experimentation. Or, to put it dramatically, in which it is measured by the distortion that is inflicted upon the materials, the forms and the structures of sensibility and thought. Postmodern is not to be taken in a periodizing sense.

given myself as an excuse for writing a political reason. I have always thought that it could be useful. Therefore, it ought to be obvious that I accept completely the notion that there is a prescriptive function to the idea of paganism. I believe that one should move in the direction that it proposes. But I am struck by the fact that prescriptives, taken seriously, are never grounded: one can never reach the just by a conclusion. And particularly, that which ought to be cannot be concluded from that which is, the "ought" from the "is." Then we are faced with one of two things: either the just comes to us from elsewhere, which means that we are never more than the addressees of prescriptions. This, by the way, is what the Jews think; it is also what obtains, though in a totally different way, in the traditions of so-called savage societies, in which traditional narratives broadcast the obligations "always" known. Or we have our situation: for us moderns, prescriptions are not received. And I think that this modernity, in the precise sense of a society that must decide what is obligatory, begins, in Western thought, with some Greeks. What does Greek mythology let us see? A society of gods that is constantly forced to redraw its code. This is a theme that one finds among several Sophists and rhetoricians. Here are people for whom prescriptions are subject to discussion, not in the sense that the discussion will lead to the more just, but rather to the extent that a prescription cannot be founded. Therefore, between statements that narrate or describe something and statements that prescribe something, there is always some talking to be done. There is a change of language game. One describes a model of strategy, of society, of economy, and then, when one passes to prescriptions, one has jumped into another language game. One is without criteria, yet one must decide.

JLT: Where does this ability to judge come from?

JFL: It bears a name in a certain philosophical tradition, namely Nietzsche's: the will to power. It is obvious that for someone like Kant (the expression "ability to judge" is Kant's), the ability to judge is left mysteriously hanging. With respect to the moral law, Kant says of the will, in the *Critique of Practical Reason*, that it is an unfathomable principle. In a way, there is nothing to say about it, that is: in truth. But, without it, there would be no experience of obligation and no problem of justice. Here is the answer then: The ability to judge does not hang upon the observance of criteria. The form that it will take in the last *Critique* is that of the imagination. An imagination that is constitutive. It is not only an ability to judge; it is a power to invent criteria.

JLT: Very good. But there is a regimen of the will, to use the term, that is that of modernity and of paganism, and another that is not, that subordinates the will to contents.

JFL: Yes, I believe that there is a possible negative discrimination: a modern will is a will (or an imagination) that does not occult itself, that does not attribute its power to a conceivable model that must be respected. Actually, there is no such thing as a classical will (when one finds one among the classics, it is modern: *virtù*): first, there are criteria, then the will models itself upon these criteria by *mimèsis*. The category of *mimèsis* prevails. But I think that it is only in classicism that it prevails. Nietzsche's attempt, successful or not, Kant's effort in the third *Critique*, are surely attempts to elaborate an ability to judge, as the latter says, to put into perspective, as the former says, and therefore to elaborate actions and discourses, works in general, without going through a conceptual system that could serve as a criterion for practice. Thus yielding works that would be modeled upon, and in conformity with, a model. This is what I call modern, and you can see that the word does not imply a historical periodization, since one can find this modernity in some ancients as well, and even among some "classics." It is obvious that someone like Pascal belongs in large part to this modernity. And "generosity" in Descartes.
. . .

JLT: I can see that, despite the absence of conceptual grounding, you are nonetheless able to decide, in every instance, saying, this is pagan, and this is not. Therefore you have a criterion. . . .

JFL: I have a criterion (the absence of criteria) to classify various sorts of discourse here and there. I have a rudimentary notion of paganism, and indeed I rely upon it in deciding. But this operation of classification belongs to a language game that has nothing to do with prescriptions: it is descriptive or denotative, as you wish; it has to do with truth functors. But we have been speaking of morality and public good. And here, I have no criteria; here we don't say, so and so is pagan but, let us be pagan—that is, we order or advise. I don't happen to think that to be pagan is the essence of human being, nor do I think that in the dialectic of history a pagan moment is now necessary after the era of religions and totalitarian sects. Neither essence nor necessity to uphold this prescription. At most, it is regulated by an Idea.

Second Day
The Three Pragmatic Positions

JLT: You often say: "Let us be pagan," and "Let us be just." Commonly, these two requirements seem to exclude each other. Indeed, justice, insofar as it is generally thought within a Platonic problematic, calls for the fixing of a criterion of judgment, which is something that paganism seems to proscribe. When you bring the two prescriptions together, are you thinking of a justice of a different type? then, what is it? Or is justice the necessary exception to paganism? then, what is the meaning of this exception? Is it the return of a nonpagan externality within paganism? And if so, why?

JFL: Ordinarily, when the problem of justice is raised, it is from a problematic of the Platonic type. It will be said that the distribution of all that circulates in a given society is just if it conforms to something defined in Plato as justice itself, that is, as the essence, or the idea, of justice. So that it is extremely difficult to conceive of what justice could be outside of the *mimèsis* of an essence of justice. Since this essence of justice must be stated by either a theoretician, or a philosopher, or a politician in the noble sense of the term, justice will be established then in conformity with the signification established in the latter's discourse. Or, again, the distribution is just if it is in conformity with a discourse that connotes just distribution. For example, for Plato, it is known that the distribution is not an egalitarian one, but rather a proportional and an analogical one.

In such a case then, the question of justice refers back to an

19

initial discourse that is descriptive, or denotative, or theoretical, to one's liking (there is no need to distinguish yet), and this discourse must be held by someone who, for some reason or other, believes that she or he is stating the very being of justice. It is quite clear that this very relation, I mean the relation of the utterer of the discourse on justice to the essence of justice, is, from my point of view, not at all pagan. To the contrary, it is deeply pious in the sense that I am trying to give to this word: it implies the representation of something that of course is absent, a lost origin, something that must be restored to a society in which it is lacking; it implies further that both the utterer and those who hear her or his utterances, that is, the entire social body, are animated in principle, and even if intermediaries are used, by a conviction, a specific *pathos*, that consists in the admission that it is indeed the being of justice that is stated in the discourse and that it serves as the basis of the just distribution. So, what is usually called justice, set in this way, and I am obviously not speaking here of its content but merely of the position of the term in a discourse that will state what that content is (that is, define justice), implies the very opposite of paganism. It implies the idea, the representation, that the thing is absent, that it is to be effected in the society, that it is lacking in the society, and that it can be accomplished only if it is first correctly thought out or described.

A just practice will have to conform to denotative statements (statements that denote justice) that are themselves true. This is where the *pathos* of the conviction is involved: it admits that the statement, of the philosopher for example, is true. This means that there is a type of discourse that somehow dominates the social practice of justice and that subordinates it to itself. This type of discourse is common to an entire political tradition (that includes Marx as well), in which it is presupposed that if the denotation of the discourse that describes justice is correct, that is, if this discourse is true, then the social practice can be just insofar as it respects the distribution implied in the discourse. I am not saying that this is sufficient of itself. Hardly anyone thinks so; otherwise there would be no need for politics. But it is in any case necessary. This is what Plato is thinking of when he speaks of the philosopher-king. The same is true of Marxism to the extent that it acknowledges the indispensable role of theory. The latter is used to carry out what has been called a "correct analysis," and that can go quite far, since it can bear upon the mode of distribution of goods called capitalism, and thus be the subject of the mighty volumes called *Das Kapital*: an enormous theoretical discourse meant to ground the legitimacy of a communist distribution of these goods.

SECOND DAY □ 21

If the problem is set in this manner, then, I will state again, we are dealing with discursive orderings whose operations are dual, something that is characteristic of the West: on the one hand, a theoretical operation that seeks to define scientifically, in the sense of the Platonic *epistémè*, or in the Marxist sense, or indeed in some other one, the object the society is lacking in order to be a good or a just society; on the other hand, plugged into this theoretical ordering, there are some implied discursive orderings that determine the measures to be taken in social reality to bring it into conformity with the representation of justice that was worked out in the theoretical discourse. So that there is, on one side, a theoretical ordering made up of denotative statements, the chief function of which is to make assertions about the reference of this discourse, and which are entirely centered upon their reference—such is for me Platonic discourse, which always sets its manifest object as its referent. On the other side, there is, paired to this ordering, a set of discourses that are implied by the previous one, at least in principle, but that differ nonetheless from it greatly, since their function is a prescriptive one with respect to social reality. They may take the form of a constitution, a set of laws, the *politéa* itself, or the orderings that Marx thinks he is discovering in the Paris Commune, for example, but that make sense only insofar as they verify, if not apply, the description that is implied in the theoretical analysis of capital.

But this type of operation, which is also that of liberalism (the latter has a general idea of what is just because it has also a certain representation of man, of humanism in general, and of individualism), this general ordering appears to be rather paradoxical when examined a little more closely. The paradox is as follows: what is implied in the ordering in question is that the prescriptive can be derived from the descriptive. I limit myself to a very schematic logical analysis, but it could easily be refined. One could observe that there is a global meta-ordering of the type: If (if P, then Q), then R. If P, then Q means: If a given distribution obtains, then justice obtains. This is theoretical discourse with its implications; this is perfectly legitimate at this level since we are in a discourse of denotative statements. Then, there is the larger *if, then* proposition, which is: If (the theoretical implication obtains), *then R*, that is, then one ought to have a just society in practice. That is, one ought to do such and such a thing, take such and such a measure, with respect to the distribution of goods, and so on.

But it has been known since Aristotle that all statements do not belong to the same class. In his *De interpretatione*, Aristotle states, with respect to request and prayers (*euchè*): All discourse is *semantikos*, but not all discourse is *apophantikos*, that is, not all discourse is proportional. And he adds that a prayer is not apophantic discourse. Now, if we replace prayer by command, since commands obviously belong to the same class of statements, that of prescriptives, we have the following: Prescriptive statements, those that I was calling *R* above, those that state: One ought to do this (eliminate family inheritance, place all banking capital in the public domain, for example), are statements that are not proportional nor predicative. But if they are not proportional, how can they be obtained through implication from propositional statements? In other words, how can one derive by means of implication commands from discourses that are not discourses of knowledge, whose function is to state the truth, and that are determinable with respect to truth or falsehood. This passage from one to the other is, properly speaking, unintelligible. There is a resistance, an incommensurability, I would say an irrelevancy, of the prescriptive with respect to the functions of propositional logic, that is, with respect to that which gives theoretical discourse to its authority (even if the clause of utterance proper to philosophical discourse is added to it).

Therefore, the vast machine of political thought that justifies itself, or believes itself to be justified, by what it wants to decree in the realm of practice so that a society be just, so that the distribution of what there is to distribute is well carried out, on the basis of a model, all this thought is actually futile, inasmuch as a command cannot find its justification in a denotative statement. This is what, for me, makes the thought of a Lévinas so important: it shows that the relation with the other, what he calls "the Other" of "the absolutely Other," is such that the request that is made of me by the other, by the simple fact that he speaks to me, is a request that can never be justified. The model here is the relation of God to the Jewish people, with God's initial statement to Moses: "Let them obey me!" At that point it is not known what is to be the content of the act of obedience; only later will it be known. First, there is this prescription to place myself in a prescriptive situation, which is actually something very strange: it is to put oneself in a condition of listening to a discourse that does not describe something but that prescribes an activity, a doing.

JLT: Let us recapitulate. You are saying that justice cannot be transcribed from ontology, that this Platonic approach ought to be dropped, and that there is an abyss between the denotative and the prescriptive.

JFL.: Plato believes that if one has a "just" (that is, true) view of being, then one can retranscribe this view into social organization, with intermediate instances, to be sure (such as the *psychè*), but nonetheless the model remains that of the very distribution of being. Society ought to repeat for itself this distribution, which will include also the distribution of assignments, responsibilities, values, goods, women, and so forth.

JLT: We ought to think of justice on the model of prayers or of requests, and not on the model of the Idea, in the Platonic sense.

JFL: When one says politics, one always means that there is something to institute. There is no politics if there is not at the very center of society, at least at a center that is not a center but everywhere in the society, a questioning of existing institutions, a project to improve them, to make them more just. This means that all politics implies the prescription of doing something else than what is. But this prescription of doing something else than what is, is prescription itself: it is the essence of a prescription to be a statement such that it induces in its recipient an activity that will transform reality, that is, the situational context, the context of the speech act. I cannot see then that, when one speaks of politics in the West, one can think of this word without bringing the prescriptive into the picture. In what is generally called the institution, in the strong sense of the term, or the instituting function, or the instituting subject, or anything of the kind, under this term of "institution" then, what is actually at stake is indeed prescription or a group of prescriptions, or a prescriptive function, or a norm-giving subject. Actually, among all these thinkers, not only Plato but Marx as well, there is the deep conviction that there is a true being of society, and that society will be just if it is brought into conformity with this true being, and therefore one can draw just prescriptions from a description that is true, in the sense of "correct." The passage from the true to the just is a passage that is the *If, then* of the example I gave.

But this passage from the true to the just raises a problem, because if one were to ground it, it would mean that a prescriptive statement would constitute an obligation only if the one who receives it, that is, the addressee of the statement, is able to put himself in the position of the sender of the statement, that is, of its utterer, in order to work out all over again the theoretical discourse that legitimates, in the eyes of this sender, the command that he is issuing. Let us consider things from this angle, that is, at the pragmatic level, I am not saying that it does not happen; generally that is what is called freedom, after all, and autonomy; I am simply saying that it leaves aside the question of how we can go . . .

JLT: . . . from the true to the just.

JFL: From the true to the just. And it also leaves to the side something else, a capital problem: insofar as I have something to do, the "doing" of this thing, I am its recipient, its addressee. There is no command except in the second person, that is, commands are explicitly addressed to their addressees. But this is rarely true of theoretical discourse, which is centered upon the referent, not upon the addressee.

JLT: In other words, you dissociate the true from the just so that the just not be subject to the critique that you have leveled at the true. This is the first operation in order to maintain, or to recast, justice.

JFL: Right. It seems to me that there is in justice, insofar as it refers to prescriptions, and it necessarily does, a use of language that is fundamentally different from the theoretical use.

JLT: There is, on this point, an unacceptable Platonic confusion.

JFL: There is a confusion that is actually political and general, but not universal, and it is a serious one: ultimately, it authorizes the privileges that philosophers have granted themselves in political matters and that they have sometimes used by becoming, for example, advisers to princes, "intellectuals," as Descartes calls them. As if a good theoretical description of a problem is what a prince needs to be able to produce correct commands.

JLT: So the just is not of the same genre as the true.

JFL: The just is not of the same genre as the true, but the word is still too fuzzy. It gains in precision if you mean by genre, genre of discourse, in the sense that Aristotle gives to the term to establish the difference between scientific and didactic discourse on the one hand, and dialectical, rhetorical, poetic discourse on the other. . . .

JLT: No, I meant it in the sense of "genres of being."

JFL: I would prefer to say classes, to be neutral, to use a logical term: there are classes of statements that, in all likelihood, do not abide by the same logical metaoperators. I know that their analysis presents very considerable difficulties. Logicians of prescription, people like von Wright, Rescher, the Anglo-Americans in general, when they try to design formalizations for prescriptive statements, begin by granting that the principal functors of propositional logic (negation, implication, etc.) also work in matters of prescription.

JLT: Then one is back in the apophantic.

JFL: Yes. This is, of course, a way of solving the problem, but it makes for a certain disappointment when one reads their books, at least as far as I am concerned. On the other hand, what interests me so much in someone like Lévinas is the forceful assertion of the original character of requests. Requests are not, and cannot be, obtained, either through deduction or implication, from denotative statements, nor calculated by means of propositional functors.

JLT: In other words, justice can be understood only from the prescriptive.

JFL: It is of the order of the prescriptive, in any case.

JLT: I mean that it cannot be thought from the theoretical and the apophantic.

JFL: That is right. The implication of this remark is that it is not a question of drawing up a model of just society. This is the first thing that must be said. The question of justice for a society cannot be resolved in terms of models. This is very important because I think that we are always tempted, whenever the question of justice arises, to go back to a model for a possible constitution, to be drawn up by a possible constitutional convention. . . .

JLT: It also means that there is no just society.

JFL: It means that there is no just society. This is a second- or third-order implication, but I believe that it could be demonstrated. I would like to add though, that this derivation of the political from the theoretical, in Plato or in Marx, for example, does not seem to hold for modern society, because the latter has an "answer" of its own to the question. In fact, it has had this answer for quite some time; it had it in Plato's day in the form of democracy, and in the form of the hypotheses on the political question formulated by some Sophists. It is an answer through autonomy; it amounts to the assertion that the set of prescriptions produced by the whole of a social body to which the prescriptions apply, will be just. In such a case, the answer does not appear to need the implication of the just from the true. Nor does it need the theoretical discourse of a specialist, or that of a group of specialists, such as philosophers or the learned ones; it does not need a discourse meant to state what justice is in order to then practice it.

JLT: There is a question I would like to ask. It may be a little simplistic, but I have the impression that this displacement of justice to the side of prescription can only lead us back to a very classical problem: morality.

JFL: Yes, but I don't think that there is any difference between the two in this respect. I state this very clearly and I think that the thinker I am closest to in this regard is Aristotle, insofar as he recognizes—and he does so explicitly in the *Rhetoric*, as well as in the *Nicomachean Ethics*, that a judge worthy of the name has no true model to guide his judgments, and that the true nature of the judge is to pronounce judgments, and therefore prescriptions, just so, without criteria. This is, after all, what Aristotle calls prudence. It consists in dispensing justice without models. It is not possible to produce a learned discourse upon what justice is. This is the difference between dialectics, for example, and the *epistemè* or didactics in Aristotle. This is tantamount to stating once again that prescriptions are not of the order of knowledge.

JLT: Yes, but I am a little bemused by the fact that in making reference to Aristotle, you are pretending to forget the other elements of his framework that correct the description you are giving of *phronèsis* [understanding], such as, for example, *héxis*, or education. To be sure, Aristotle's judge does judge without criteria, does judge without any theoretical purport that permits the fixation of the just, but that is because he has been educated, because there is a habit, because there is a pedagogy of the soul.

JFL: I am not even sure that one can say that.

JLT: Aristotle would say that there is virtue at least.

JFL: Yes, but virtue will manifest itself in the fact that judgments pronounced outside of criteria are judgments that are just. This is how one will know that a judge is a good judge. It is not because a judge is virtuous that he will judge justly, but if he does judge justly one will be able to say that he is virtuous.

JLT: You don't feel that Aristotle would say that it is because he has been given the habit of being virtuous, that is, because he has a just *éthos*?

JFL: It is true that he speaks of an *éthos*. . . . But what is this *éthos*? Ultimately, it is a description, an empirical and not a theoretical one this time, but still a description of what someone who always holds to the just mean can be. Which is precisely to say that the good *éthos* of the judge, far from being the cause of just judgments, is that which can manifest itself only through just judgments.

JLT: But once again, you are pretending to forget, it seems to me, and this notion of "mean" brings it to mind, that there is a theoretical framework in place here: the calculation of the mean.

JFL: I don't think that one can say that this calculation is theoretical. It is a calculation that bears upon objects for which there is no truth. In other words, these are statements about possibilities, and statements about possibilities are only statements of opinion. The judge relies upon opinions.

JLT: We are in dialectics.

JFL: We are in dialectics, and we are never in the *epistémè*. I think that dialectics is all the prescriptive authorizes. I mean by this that dialectics cannot present itself as producing a model that would be a model that would be valid once and for all for the constitution of the social body. On the contrary, dialectics allows the judge to judge case by case. But if he can, and indeed must (he has no choice), judge case by case, it is precisely because each situation is singular, something that Aristotle is very sensitive to. This singularity comes from the fact that we are in matters of opinion and not in matters of truth. So much so that the *éthos* of the judge indicates that an ethics of reasonable distribution has been constituted. And the reason implied in this reasonableness has nothing to do with Plato's reason; it is not a reason that states being. It is a reason that is an understanding, in Weber's sense, for example (not at all a *Vernunft*; it is a *Verstand*.) It is a calculating reason, as in strategy; it is a mode of strategy, but one in which the issue is not how to conquer but how to achieve parity between people. This is the difference. In every instance, one must evaluate relations: of force, of values, of quantities, and of qualities; but to evaluate them there are no criteria, nothing but opinions.

JLT: But it does seem to me that with the notion of mean we do have a theoretical statement that is used as a criterion for justice: In every instance one chooses the mean. The aleatory estimating calculation is concerned only with the determination of this mean.

JFL: When one says: in every instance, choose the mean, it means, for Aristotle, that this mean cannot be determined in itself, that is, outside of the situation in which we find it. In fact, regarding this mean, when we speak of it, we really are not saying anything that we can even conceive of, before it is determined in a concrete case. The idea of a mean is not a concept. The mean functions more like an idea, I would almost say, an idea of the understanding, than a determining concept. Unable to define once and for all, *à la* Plato, since there is no "once and for all" here, we just have an idea to guide us. This is characteristic of the judge's position.

JLT: To be sure, the difference between Plato's, and Aristotle's, conception of justice is quite apparent, and one could indeed draw up an Aristotelian theory of justice. But what is problematic to me is the relation between an Aristotelian theory of justice and paganism.

When you are describing Aristotle's judge, are you speaking of paganism? Is that where we must leave things?

JFL: I believe that the Aristotle of the *Politics*, of the *Ethics*, even of the *Topics* and the *Rhetoric*, is indeed an Aristotle very close to paganism. I choose these different books deliberately because, in every one of them, we deal with a discourse that attempts to establish the good *tekhnè*, the art and not the knowledge, in a matter in which there cannot be any knowledge because we are deep in opinions, Politics belongs to this sphere; it does not belong to the sphere of knowledge.

JLT: It belongs to dialectics and not to science.

JFL: This is how I would define what interests me in paganism: It is the conviction that, with respect to all these matters at least, we are always in judgments of opinion and not in judgments of truth.

JLT: Yes, there is no science of the political.

JFL: Therefore, there is no science of the political. I would put it otherwise: There is no metalanguage, and by metalanguage, I mean the famous theoretical discourse that is supposed to ground political and ethical decisions that will be taken as the basis of its statements.

JLT: There is no metalanguage; there are only genres of language, genres of discourse.

JFL: Yes. One works "case by case" even when one is producing a constitution; after all, it can only be implemented in the light of practice, that is, one will realize that practice constitutes a new context for the statements of the constitution, and that this context requires that such and such a thing be prescribed, which had not been prescribed in the constitution, and the latter is therefore amended. In this sense, I think that, inasmuch as there is no reference to the presumption of a metalanguage that is shaping society in conformity to itself, one can say that there is paganism whenever there is this very curious representation wherein he who states the just is himself as caught in the very sphere of language as those who will be the recipients of his prescriptions, and may eventually be judged by the judge. The judge is in the same sphere of language, which means that he will be considered just only by his actions, if it can be seen that he judges well, that he is really just. And he will really be just only if his actions are just. And his actions can be judged to be just only when one adds up all the accounts. But in matters of opinion there is no adding up of accounts, no balance sheet.

JLT: I wonder whether Aristotle formulates this idea of the "case by case" as radically as you do. He does suppose that, as one makes just decisions, one is more and more just, and that there is therefore a cumulative effect.

JFL: Yes, there is such an effect, and in fact it belongs to the very logic of opinion. We are not in the *always* here, but in the *often*. And therefore if the judge judges well very often, one will say that there is a presumption that she is just, but one cannot say she will always be just. Never is it always. Paganism admits readily that there are some people more just than others because they have often judged justly.

JLT: Is it that you are an Aristotelian?

JFL: One finds in Aristotle a way of setting the problem that seems interesting to me, because I think that it is pagan, at that level and for that part of his work. As far as metaphysics and physics are concerned, it may be another matter, though one could show, as Aubenque did, that, after all, even the ontological is always stated in a discourse that, in the final analysis, is dialectical, and that ontology is an impossible science if it is to be a theoretical discourse that states the truth on being. It is possible otherwise; it is possible as dialectic, that is, precisely as not a science.

JLT: You are an Aristotelian.

JFL: Yes, if this is how Aristotle is interpreted. It is as if he knew very well that all the important things with respect to the social body or the social bond belong to dialectics, and occur within the order of opinion, and not in the order of truth. I think that this is quite close to some of the themes that one finds among the Sophists.

JLT: Let us return now, if you will, to the answer that modernity gives to the question of justice, namely, the answer of autonomy.

JFL: In modernity, let us say since Rousseau, the answer to the question of justice in relation to theoretical discourse, is displaced, because it has been thought that the just will be that which can be prescribed by the set of the utterers of the statements. The position is quite different from the Platonic one, because what the utterers state does not necessarily offer any guidance, in such a perspective. I would even say that it is not necessarily guided by the denotation of a model of good distribution.

JLT: You are probably alluding to the emergence of the notion of the will in modernity.

JFL: I am talking about the emergence of enunciation itself. From the *Cogito* or the *Volo* (and without distinguishing between the two), whether in Descartes or elsewhere, and in Rousseau no less explicitly but in a different way, we are dealing with a notion that does not exist in Plato: the ability that you call the will in general, and that I would rather call the enunciating capability.

JLT: I am calling it "will" because the history of philosophy sees its appearance as characteristic of modernity. I was thinking specifically of the Introduction to the *Principles of the Philosophy of Right.*

JFL: If you will. This type of will does not exist in Platonism; it does not even exist in Aristotle. But it does exist in those philosophies in which the subject of the enunciation, as it has been called (insofar as it exists, which is something I have my doubts about), is placed in a locus where ultimately it will be the one to issue prescriptions. The question then becomes: Which is the subject of the enunciation? This is a very important displacement as far as the political problematic is concerned. It gets us out of the problematic of the model, in the Platonic sense of the term, and, by the same token, out of the two-stage framework I was talking about earlier, namely, the framework "denotative discourse stating the true on the social bond, and prescriptive discourse implied in the previous type of discourse." Instead, one gets into a problematic in which the main issue is that of a subject who is at once the sender and the addressee of the prescription, the statement of foremost concern to ethics and politics. The Kant of the second *Critique* belongs to this problematic. At least, he also belongs to it (for Kant is also bound to a different language game, much less "modern" and much more "Jewish.") Here one finds something that is already opposed to the previous model, a model in which imperatives were constructed hypothetically as in the form *If P, then R*. Now the imperatives have a categorical form, and they are categorical only inasmuch as the will, in the Kantian sense, is autonomous in the utterance of the law. And so we get to this idea of autonomy that has dominated, and still dominates, the modern problematic of politics and of justice.

JLT: And one gets back to the question that I was raising earlier; morality and its relations to justice.

JFL: Absolutely. Within this problematic, one will say that a statement is just if it can be uttered by all the wills, inasmuch as in uttering it, these wills do not alienate their freedom.

JLT: And so justice is defined without recourse to science.

JFL: Yes, without recourse to science.

JLT: But that does not make it pagan, I think.

JFL: No, it does not, far from it. The principle here is that of autonomy, the autonomy of the will, that is, the autonomy of the subject who states the law, and who remains autonomous even when he obeys it since he is its author. A whole slew of categories comes to the fore then: responsibility, authority, etc. One is the author of the law that one pays heed to, and justice will obtain only inasmuch as distribution is carried out by the subject of the enunciation who is a free subject.

JLT: It is not enough, then, to dissociate the true from the just to get paganism.

JFL: Indeed not. Let me insist a little more on this business of autonomy because, as you well know, this is a theme that is the object of a certain amount of renewal of interest in various movements of that name in Italy and in Germany, movements that, insofar as they use the word autonomy in their names, are implicated in, or concerned by, this problematic of a subject who is the author of a law. An autonomous group—and I do know that the word is not meant this way, that it refers to the group's independence from parliamentary parties, such a group is, in the final analysis and upon examination of its writings, a group that believes that justice lies in the self-determination of peoples. In other words, there is a close relation between autonomy and self-determination: one gives oneself one's own laws.

As you say, this is obviously not paganism. On the contrary, in paganism, there is the intuition, the idea—in the almost Kantian sense of the term, if I may say so—that is, the idea that no maker of statements, no utterer, is ever autonomous. On the contrary, an utterer is always someone who is first of all an addressee, and I would even say one destined. By this I mean that he is someone who, before he is the utterer of a prescription, has been the recipient of a prescription, and that he is merely a relay; he has also been the object of a prescription. To determine paganism then, one needs not only to oppose it to the theory of the model, to give this name to the theory that one finds in Plato, but one must also oppose it to the theory of autonomy. (As far as the political plane is concerned, this is where I have broken away from the notion of self-management, a notion that seems to me to belong entirely to this problematic of the subject of the enunciation.) In order to apprehend what is really pagan, as a sphere, as a field, I would even say as a field of social and political experimentation, one must go back once more to discourse pragmatics and see how they work in the field of paganism. We can be sure that this functioning never involves the category of autonomy.

Let me take up the example of the Cashinahua, Indians from the upper Amazon, who have been discussed by André Marcel d'Ans in his *Dit des vrais hommes* [Sayings of True Men]. This is a collection of narratives of various kinds: some are sacred narratives, transmitted in fixed form and in a sung and ritual fashion, while others are profane narratives told upon request, and their teller increases the number of rhetorical devices to make them more striking. There are thus two extremes. But in all cases, whenever a story is told in this ethnic group, the teller always begins by saying: "I am going to tell you the story of X (here he inserts the name of the hero) as I have always heard it." And then he adds: "Listen to it!" In other words, he presents himself without giving his own name; he only relays the story. He presents himself as having first been the addressee of a story of which is he now the teller.

Every narrator presents himself as having first been a narratee: not as autonomous, then, but, on the contrary, as heteronomous. The law of his narrative, if I can speak of law in such a case, is a law that is has received. It is only at the end of the story—which he always ends by saying: "Here ends the story of X; it was told to you by Y"—that his name is given, or rather his double name: his Cashinahua name and his name in Spanish or in Portuguese, depending on whether he is registered in Peru or in Brazil, since the Cashinahua territory straddles the border. It is only at that moment that his name as a narrator, his proper name, is given. After, and not before. And what is striking is that when one of the listeners takes up the story some other time, he "forgets" the name of the previous narrator, since he does not give the name of the narrator who came before. One has "always heard it told." It should be added that the proper name, the Cashinahua one, is an esoteric one that allows the localization of the speaker in an extremely exact, and far more formal than real, network of kinship relations. So that, when he gives his proper name, the teller designates himself as someone who has been narrated by the social body, in a narrative that includes proper names and in which he has a place of his own. Among the stories he tells, there is also this story.

In the *Dit des vrais hommes*, one can find narratives on the origins of marriage moieties, which are actually groups of eight people, men and women, with a system of oppositions, that regulate marriage exchanges and define kinship relations. Which means that the teller sees himself at once as the addressee of these narratives and as the subject matter of some others that define the social bonds in the form of kinship relations. In saying at the beginning, "I am going to tell you what I have always heard," and at the end, "My name is so-and-so," he situates himself in the two forgotten poles—actively forgotten, repressed—of Western thought and of the tradition of autonomy. Those are the poles where one is the recipient of a narrative in which one is narrated, and where one receives a narrative that has been narrated to one. That is, where one is oneself on the side of the reference of the narrative, where one has been part of the action of this narrative while still being so-and-so in the Cashinahua system; and also where one has been on the addressee pole of the narrative, where one is in the position of listener. This is an essential feature of paganism, in my view, and it is probably what has been the most eradicated in Western thought, not only in Plato, but also in Kant (inasmuch as he succumbs to the fascination of autonomy). Here we are in a mode of transmission of discourse that elaborates itself through its insistence on the pole of reference (the one who speaks is someone who has been "spoken") and on the pole of the narratee (the one who speaks is someone who has been spoken to). The subject of the enunciation makes no claims of autonomy with respect to his discourse. On the contrary, both through his name and through the story he tells, he claims to belong to the tradition.

JLT: This vaunted paganism would be nothing but the tradition, then.

JFL: But paganism is the tradition. And I believe that this is a point on which we have to completely reverse our Western ethnocentric thought. I don't think that the tradition signifies at all, as it is generally said, a relation to time that would be a relation of preservation in which the important thing would be to keep things from being used up by time, and to reject the new. In fact, and André Marcel d'Ans underscores this, the teller expends vast amounts of poetic and rhetorical inventiveness, including of course plays on words, jokes, and even mime, to animate his narrative. At that level, what we would call the "artistic" one, these Indians are extraordinarily productive, and they are quite capable of telling good storytellers apart from indifferent ones. The relevant feature is not faithfulness: it is not because one has preserved the story well that one is a good narrator, at least as far as profane narratives are concerned. On the contrary, it is because one "hams" it up, because one invents, because one inserts novel episodes that stand out as motifs against the narrative plot line, which, for its part, remains stable, that one is successful. When we say tradition, we think identity without difference, whereas there actually is very much difference: the narratives get repeated but are never identical. This whole problem has generally been avoided by someone like Lévi-Strauss, through a structuralist approach, in which it is treated as a problem of variants.

Why are there variants? It is a surprising thing. Is it a case of entropy, or is it a case of experimentation? I tend to think that it is a matter of experimentation. Even the fact that the same narrative plots recur, what does that mean? It is not by chance that popular narratives become extremely simple (proverbs, moralities); they become almost pure discourse rhythms, as in "Like father, like son," or "A rolling stone gathers no moss," etc., in which the proximity to music is quite apparent, and not only because of the frequent rhymes, but because there are matters of rhythmic phenomena in language that are reminiscent of *Sprachgesang* [recitative]. What matters in the transmission of these narratives, in the repetition of their narrational etiquette, is to tell while being a relay; it is to be the (traditional) bearer of the narrative because, in the simple fact of relaying something, there is precisely something that gets forgotten.

Tradition needs to be rethought. I am thinking of some of Daniel Charles's remarks in *Le Temps de la voix* [*In Voice's Time*], as well as of some of John Cage's, that explain the enormous power of so-called repetitive musics: It lies in the fact that they cause the forgetting of what is being repeated and they make for a nonforgetting of time as a beat in place. Tradition is that which concerns time, not content. Whereas what the West wants from autonomy, invention, novelty, self-determination, is the opposite—to forget time and to preserve, acquire, and accumulate contents. To turn them into what we call history, and to think that it progresses because it accumulates. On the contrary, in the case of popular traditions, and I think that this is universal and not something limited to the Cashinahua, nothing gets accumulated, that is, the narratives must be repeated all the time because they are forgotten all the time. But what does not get forgotten is the temporal beat that does not stop sending the narratives to oblivion.

I believe that this feature is deeply pagan. This relation to time that is so astonishing that it has led us to make the most preposterous statements about societies without history, gets translated into a pragmatics whose chief effect is that no discourse presents itself as autonomous, but always as a discourse that has been received. Consequently, the narratives, with their own rhythms, are narratives that are borne, if I may say so, by themselves on the mouths and through the ears of the people of these societies; they get forgotten along the way, and therefore they repeat themselves like the repetitive musics, and their repetition does no more than mark the beat *proteron/*

usteron, one/two, one/two, which is the dyad, the simplest of the metric elements. More generally, I would say, at the level of what linguistics call discourse pragmatics, and more specifically, with respect to the pragmatics of narrative discourses, which strike me more and more as the popular form of discourse, I would say that people get into language not by speaking it but by hearing it. And what they hear as children is stories, and first of all their own story, because they are named in it. This implies the very opposite of autonomy: heteronomy. It also implies that, ultimately, it is not true that a people can ever give itself its own institutions.

JLT: It seems to me that you are rediscovering a question of classical politics: that of the lawgiver. Human beings have never been able to, it is said, give themselves their own laws. The laws must have come from elsewhere.

JFL: No, that is not it. First, I rediscover the question of the prescriptive, or rather that of the addressee of the prescriptive, insofar as any Cashinahua (as André Marcel d'Ans makes clear in his excellent, though differently oriented, account) having heard a story is bound to retell it, because, to refuse to retell it would mean that he does not want to share, which is something that has a very derogatory name in Cashinahua and is a great abomination to them. In other words, someone speaks to me; he places me under an obligation. This is precisely what Lévinas has been thinking. What kind of obligation? The obligation to retell. But not necessarily to my teller. I am not obligated to give it back to him, no, that is not it; but I am obligated in the way of a relay that may not keep its charge but must pass it on. I don't think that this is the question of the lawgiver in the sense that you raised it. I know that it is the question of prescription in the sense that there is a kind of imperative in which, as soon as I have been spoken to as well as spoken of (in the sense that I have a name, etc.) I have to speak. And in this sense, the will is never free, and freedom does not come first. That I may say something else later, granted; that then there is will, granted. But this will can be exercised only against the backdrop of an obligation that comes first and is much older, much more archaic, and it is not subject to legislations; it has not been the object of a decree; and it is literally anonymous. When you say: But this is Plato's problem, or, this is Rousseau's problem; human beings must get their legislation from elsewhere, I would reply that this is a somewhat imaginary, and rather rapidly metaphysical, view of a fact that is not metaphysical but physical, namely, the fact that stories are animated with movement and that as they pass over you, you must pass the movement on. I would make it the subject of a kinetic metaphor: it is a kind of energy transmission. But this transmission obviously takes place in the mode of prescription. There is movement to be passed on. It seems to me that we are dealing here with something that is pagan insofar as it is essential to paganism to acknowledge heteronomy. But the "elsewhere" from which the prescription to pass on narratives comes is immanent to the narrative pragmatics itself.

Heteronomy implies that the marked pole is not at all the pole of the author, which explains why narratives are anonymous. I must say that all this intrigues me. Why do we find it natural — and we always seem to find it natural — that the first narratives, that the oldest narratives we know, are anonymous? It is not by chance; it is because the pole of the author is not the most important one, something we find almost unthinkable today. And the poles selected are the other two poles of the narratives triangle: the pole of reference and the pole of the addressee. This heteronomy is essential to paganism inasmuch as paganism is not atheism but implies rather that there are gods. Which means, as the content of the narratives makes abundantly clear anyway, that human beings are not the authors of what they tell, that is, of what they do, and that, in point of fact, there never are authors. Which does not mean that they have nothing to do. On the contrary, they have a thousand things to do, and they must constantly match wits with the fate they have been given, as well as with the fate they are being given in being made the addressee of any given speech act, such as an oracle, or a dream, for instance. It is precisely because they are not the authors of meaning that they must always rely on their wits. We are never in the autonomy of power.

JLT: I think that one could further specify that these notions of autonomy and heteronomy can appear and function only in a determinate "genre" of discourse, as, for example, one could speak of the "genre" of the narrative that is privileged by paganism, and that excludes, as a discursive "genre," the question of autonomy or that of heteronomy. Could not one say then that, to every "poetics" there corresponds a politics, in the sense in which by "poetics" one means the fact that a discourse is focused on such and such a pole.

JFL: Absolutely. There is a discourse that is indeed centered on the subject of the enunciation, that is, in fact, on the pole of the utterer. . . .

JLT: In such a case, we have autonomy and heteronomy. . . .

JFL: Yes, you get autonomy, self-determination, the *Cogito*, the *Ich denke*, etc.; you get all the thought centered on the speaking subject, a subject that speaks, that does, and that causes to do. And this pole happens to be also the speculative pole. What is philosophical discourse, at least the modern kind? It is a denotative discourse that differs from that of the sciences by the fact that the subject of the enunciation constantly works itself into the discourse by means of specific clauses. To a scientist it is an impure discourse inasmuch as it is not strictly denotative but is infiltrated all the time by modalizations that imply the presence of a subject of the enunciation. Hegel is perfectly clear on this subject. Insofar as the discourse is denotative, it is substance, but insofar as the subject of the enunciation is present in it, it is subject. And when Hegel says that what is needed is a substance that is also subject, he says very clearly what philosophical discourse is. Philosophical discourse, even if it is denotative, inasmuch as it is infiltrated by enunciation, belongs to the pole of autonomy. To continue now this general review of illocutionary instances, as Searle calls them, and to indicate the locus in which the discourse is active, I would say that the absolute privileging of the pole of the addressee, as the only site in which the social body can hold, is to be found in Jewish thought. By which I mean the thought of Lévinas. It marks the place where something is prescribed to me, that is, where I am obligated before any freedom.

JLT: When you speak of a discourse that privileges the addressee above all, I think you should indicate that in such a case the question of autonomy or heteronomy does not arise.

JFL: Not at all.

JLT: It needs to be specified, otherwise it may be understood as servitude.

JFL: It is not servitude at all, because this is prior to the question of freedom. It is what Lévinas calls *passivity* (a theme I have a liking for, with its value of provocation), and of which he says that it is obviously prior to what may pass for passivity once free choices must be made.

JLT: Otherwise it would be but more thinking within our usual and habitual political framework of autonomy and heteronomy.

JFL: I agree entirely. This is very important. I would also add that this pole, this very strange privilege granted to the pole of the addressee, is something that is forgotten, actively forgotten, in Western thought. What you are saying shows exactly how it has been forgotten and how it has been rejected, that is, it has been purely and simply assimilated. To assimilate with servitude the hold placed upon me by the discourse's address, a hold that is an obligation, that puts me into movement, this is the West's way of repressing, rejecting, and smearing, the privilege granted to the pole of the addressee, quite in keeping with the West's way of spitting on the Jews. It is roughly the same thing. This is a very important point because I think that what we were saying earlier alluded to it, far more in fact than to Aristotle.

JLT: This distinction between passivity and servitude seems to me to be tied to the status of the speaker. Because if the latter is something like the *Cogito*, then I fall into servitude, I think we should specify the nature of the speaker in the case of Judaism.

JFL: This is a very good question. But first, if you will, a last word on the third pole and on the importance that, paradoxically enough, is given to it in a pragmatic configuration: Even s/he who speaks can speak only inasmuch as s/he is spoken [of]. This is the pragmatics of the narrative of popular tales.

JLT: It does not apply to Yahweh.

JFL: It definitely does not apply to Yahweh.

JLT: One cannot say that he speaks inasmuch as he is spoken.

JFL: Just so. We have these three orderings: autonomy, which is characteristic of Western thought and can be found all over the political plane. Then we have another ordering that is poorly known but constantly used and exploited, insofar as it represents an essential form of the social bond, which is the ordering of obligation, that is, it is the one that valorizes the pole of the addressee of the message. This is the Jewish pole. And then there is a third ordering that is popular, properly pagan, "peasant" in the sense of pagan (and not the reverse): the people of the *pagus* (who are not the people of the village), who do any telling only inasmuch as it has been told, and who, themselves, are told in what they tell. This pole is repressed under the form of ethnology, of folklore, with the idea that it is a primitive state of discourse from which we have managed to get out by means of some well-known operations, basically Platonic ones—I am thinking here of the (unsuccessful) repression of poets and myths attempted in the Republic. The myths, for example, are classed as old wives' tales that have no truth value. Which actually is quite true, since they do not have any truth value in the sense of speculative discourse. But they have a pragmatic value by the same token as the statements valorized by the other orderings. We have thus these three poles.

Now, you are asking me: What about the "one who speaks" in

the case of Judaism? The core of Lévinas's thought on this, is that the one who speaks is always the other, without a capital *o*. It is always the one who is speaking to me, and inasmuch as he is issuing prescriptions to me or asking me something while talking to me, I cannot put myself in his place. The place of the one who speaks to me is never available to me to occupy, since his request cannot come from me. If one takes the Talmud, for example, one can note that it is always a matter of taking up speech again from a text that one has heard, and, at the same time, that one has not heard. And it is for that reason that one must take up speech again, because it is, in a certain way, inaudible. One will have to speak then on something that one has heard but not understood. What is at stake here for the speaking subject is his status of relay, of "commentator," in relation to something that is told to him and that he will never hear out entirely. And he must never pass over to the position of the one who speaks, that is, he must never assume the authority that the one who addressed him is supposed to have with respect to the meaning at hand.

JLT: Yes, and it is for that reason that in this type of relation to speech, insofar as I cannot put myself in the position of the speaker, the issue of autonomy, as well as that of heteronomy, do not arise, and indeed are meaningless. For the sake of comparison, would it be possible to sketch a parallel to the mythologies of the Greek Pantheon?

JFL: What is important in the case of the Greeks is that their gods are not masters of the word in the sense in which the Christian God is a master of the word, that is, their word is not performative as the word of the Christian God is. It does not create the world, nor does it create any of the situations of the world, even though a given god may have such a power, in an oracle, for example.

What is very important is that among the pagans, these gods, even when they have the position of first speaker, are themselves narrated in narratives that tell what they are telling. This relation—an intradiegetic relation—means that the one who speaks is at the same time the hero of a story in which he is narrated himself; and these embeddings can be multiplied without end. It is, mutatis mutandis, the same situation as that of the Cashinahua narrator in relation to the story he tells since he narrates the story, I repeat, from a position where he is himself narrated, where he knows himself to be narrated. This is a situation of continuous embedding, which makes it impossible to find a first utterer. And this is the situation that recurs in the case of Ulysses: Ulysses is the hero of a narrative that is Homer's narrative, but, in addition, on the stage of the *Odyssey*, Ulysses, while a guest at the court of Alkinoos, tells the story of his previous adventures, stories of which he is the hero and which he tells in Homer's place; he is at once narrated by Homer and a narrator like Homer. So that, in a way, Ulysses, telling his adventures, also tells how Homer tells his, Ulysses', return.

These stories have no origin. They treat origins in terms of stories that presuppose other stories that in turn presuppose the first ones. And so the gods can become, like human beings, like Ulysses, the heroes of numerous, almost innumerable, narratives, all set into each other. They become like a species of proper names whose corresponding bodies change. In some respects, this is a sort of pagan ideal that occurs again and again in various forms, including in the religions of the late Roman Empire. This is the ideal of games and masks: the awareness that the relation between the proper name and the body is not an immutable one. This bars the way to the very notion of a subject identical to itself through the peripeteia of its history. There is no subject because s/he changes bodies, and by changing bodies, s/he, of course, changes passions as well as functions, especially narrative ones. There will be a multiplicity of functions for the same proper name. As a result it will turn out to be quite difficult to draw up a functional organizational chart of the Greek Olympus, because so many of the functions are interchangeable.

JLT: With the reservation that one can take hold of Proteus nonetheless, even though it is more difficult and more complicated. But it is still feasible.

JFL: To take hold of him? How?

JLT: Literally, by grabbing him so that he can conform to his identity. One gets back to the notion that the gods are subject to the same treatment as human beings, to persuasion or ruse. . . .

JFL: Definitely. They may be defeated but not once for all. There is always present the idea, and it is a pagan one, that if one has overcome the gods, that is, a metamorphic form that is difficult to name because it is difficult to recognize in its mask, which is its body, then that is the moment of greatest peril, because the relation one has to the gods is one of weak to strong, and one can expect some form of reprisal. At the moment of victory one has been imprudent. It is imprudent to win.

JLT: And it is extremely dangerous, and imprudent, not to recognize a god in a different guise.

JFL: Definitely. It is imprudent to overcome because that may lead the god to think that one has not recognized him or her since one has overcome, whereas s/he is the stronger. There is a relation here that is specifically pagan, that is to be found in all popular traditions: measure or moderation. Clastres was saying this about the Guayaki; Lévi-Strauss saw it among the Nambikwara; and it is readily apparent among the Cashinahua, especially in their relation to the forest, an ecological relation as we would call it now, a relation that is extremely moderate and modest, that never seeks to conquer. When one cuts a sort of field in the forest, one does not exhaust, one does not destroy everything, one leaves some trees. It is more prudent to let the forces of the forest cooperate rather than make them surrender and then risk their return in some form or other. It is always a relation of struggle, of conflict, that occurs in all the stories, but at the same time, there are ruses of moderation. It is not a question of conquest at any price; rather it is a matter of making a show of force, a show of one's strength instead of conquering. Instead of reducing the opponent to silence, it is better to have him acknowledge that one is subtle.

I think that one can carry this relation over to the level of narrative pragmatics, by which I mean that there is to be found in this pragmatics the same moderation, the same ruse: a narrative that has been handed down is picked up and will be passed on in such a way as to remain recognizable. But it will undergo a metamorphosis in the way that it will be given. It will not be a matter of conquering the narrative, that is, of putting oneself forward as the utterer, and imprinting one's name on it. That would be quite crude and a mistake. If the privileged pole of this relation is that of the narrated, it is not because these people are concerned only with the contents of what they tell, but because the one doing the speaking speaks in the place of the referent. As narrator, s/he is narrated as well. And, in a way, s/he is already told, and what s/he him/herself is telling will not undo the fact that somewhere else s/he is told, but it will "ruse" with this; it will offer a variant in the form and even in the story. Then, there is a relation of dependency. But this relation of dependency is not the same one that one finds in Judaism, to get back to it. I would not say: It does not matter what is told; but when Lévinas, citing a much-commented-on passage of the Talmud, says: "Do before you understand, and the Jews did, and then they understood," he sets the problem exactly right. It is clear that it is not a question of first understanding, no! First, one acts from the obligation that comes from the simple fact that I am being spoken to, that you are speaking to me, and then, and only then, can one try to understand what has been received. In other words, the obligation operator comes first and then one sees what one is obligated to.

JLT: In paganism, the gods do not speak.

JFL: The gods do not speak to me, even when I consult them. As they say, they signify, they do not speak. It cannot be said that the gods speak to me, certainly not in the Jewish sense.

JLT: In the case of the oracle, one could say that the gods speak to me but as a human being does, that is, with the same degree of uncertainty, of deception, of ruse, and of chance, that obtains in any human exchange.

JFL: Yes, that is so. And their oracles are always very dangerous because they lend themselves to misunderstanding. There is no truthfulness, in fact, quite the contrary. In Apollo's oracle defining Oedipus' fate, the utterance is focused on the narrated, which means that the Oedipus who is seen on the stage, Sophocles' Oedipus, is already someone who belongs to a narratitve, to the narrative that Apollo has made of him. He finds himself therefore in the pagan situation of having a kind of "fate" inflicted upon him by this utterance. But I think that we misunderstand completely when we turn this into a tragedy of consciousness or of the instincts, because I think that for the Greeks, this oracle is to be taken, as you have said, with prudence, with measure, perhaps even with humor. In some respects, Oedipus is a comic character, especially insofar as he remains "stuck" to Apollo's text and that he does not know how to tell a story that would put forward a variant of the story in which he himself is narrated, that is, of which he is the hero. He does not know how to ruse as a narrator with the story of which he is the hero. This is his flaw. I am more and more convinced that this must have been a source of comedy to the Greeks. Of course, it must have frightened them as well, but one does not exclude the other. It was worrisome but certainly astonishing because the relation of the gods to human beings is not at all like that. There is always the possibility of relating things differently.

In other words, I think that the relation between gods and humans is to be thought of in terms of boundaries. And *pagus* always indicates the country, the region. It is the opposite of *Heim*, of "home," that is, of the village. It is quite a beautiful word since it gave us *pax*, "companion," etc. It is the place where one *compacts* with something else. (It is the same root. From time to time, let us allow ourselves some parodic etymologies; this one happens to be "true" in any case.) It is a place of boundaries. Boundaries are not borders. And the relation with the gods, including the pragmatic relation of discourses, does not obey a pragmatics of border to border, between the two perfectly defined blocks or two armies, or two verbal sets, confronting each other. On the contrary, it is a place of ceaseless negotiations and ruses. Which means that there is no reference by which to judge the opponent's strength; one does not know if s/he is a god or a human. It is a beggar, but it may be a god, since the other is metamorphic, and one will have to judge therefore by opinion alone, that is, without criteria. And here I get back to Aristotle. We are always within opinion, and there is no possible discourse of truth on the situation. And there is no such discourse because one is caught up in a story, and one cannot get out of this story to take up a metalinguistic position from which the whole could be dominated. We are always immanent to stories in the making, even when we are the ones telling the story to the other.

JTL: In the same way that the gods are immanent to the stories of which they are the elements, the objects.

JFL: Absolutely. There are sets of narratives . . .

JLT: . . . from which they can never get out.

JFL: Right.

JLT: And the proof lies in the fact that they fight with humans, they get injured. . . . If they were true gods, they should know that they will get injured by humans . . . or they should not get injured at all.

JFL: But they are not gods in that sense at all. They are not all-knowing. They just have their stories, that humans do not know. And humans have their own stories. And these two sets of stories are, if you will, not two blocks but two centers that send out their elements to negotiate, if one can call it that, on the boundaries. This is paganism. One does not know whom one is speaking to; one must be very prudent; one must negotiate; one must ruse; and one must be on the lookout when one has won.

JLT: Because there is no outside.

JFL: Right, there is no outside; there is no place from which one could photograph the whole thing.

JLT: The gods are implicated in the narratives.

JFL: This is the implication I have been calling the privilege granted to the pole of the narratee.

Third Day
A General Literature

JLT: We have seen that it is illusory to seek to ground prescriptive statements, and that it is not proper to derive them from another class of statements, namely, from theoretical statements. Nevertheless, I will still ask, perhaps rather stubbornly, if these statements cannot be derived, why are they kept? In other words, why must one be just? For indeed, even if we do not know what it is to be just, the prescription of a "must," of an "ought" is kept.

JFL: First, "must" and "ought" are not quite the same thing. "Must" is "you must," while "ought" is a "you must" already grafted onto an ontology, even if it be an anti-ontology, as with Nietzsche. This having been said, and in spite of the Scholastic distinctions, when you ask "Why ought we be just?" it is a serious question. You take the "you must" and you cite it, if I may say so, in a question, in a sort of interrogational descriptive, namely: Why the "you must"? Why keep, to use your word, the "you must"? When you ask this type of question, you are taking things the way philosophers or metaphysicians have always taken them, because you are demanding of me a descriptive discourse, or the genre of descriptive discourse that is called "speculative" and comes with utterance clauses and operators characteristic of philosophical discourse. Such discourse, among other things, claims to justify the "you must," that is, the existence of undetermined prescriptions, in Kant's phrase, and thus the existence of obligation in general. So, what you are asking me to do is to deduce obligation. This I cannot undertake since it has already been said—Kant has tried to say it in part in the second *Critique*, and Lévinas has said it—that it is proper to prescription to be left hanging in midair, if I may put it thus. Any discourse meant to account for prescriptions, transforms them into conclusions of reasonings, into propositions derived from other propositions, in which the latter are metaphysical propositions on being and history, or on the soul, or on society. In such a derivation, or deducation, or prescriptions, what is derived or deduced is not the prescriptive itself but the citation of the prescriptive, that is, the image, the representation, in the linguistic sense, of the prescriptive: it is not "you must," it is the "you must," that there be some "you must." But the proper of the prescriptive is that it . . . (I was about to say, "antecedes") anticipates or at least precedes its own image.

In the final analysis, your question supposes that it is possible to derive prescriptives, prescription, obligation in general, and the "you must" as such. That is, not the content ("you must do this" or "you must do that") but the fact of the "you must," that there be some "you must," in its pragmatic existence. To which I say: It cannot be derived. The question you are asking is that of the relation between two language games: that of prescription and that of description (whether speculative or not). The description of the "you must," the prescription: "you must." This is a point that, for me, shines clearly: to establish a derivation between the two is to tie in with the tradition of the intellectual, with the tradition of a form of thought that is there to try to justify imperatives whatever they may be. And the fact that they may be imperatives in keeping with dominant morality (inasmuch as there is one) or in keeping with the dominant political power, or, to the contrary, that they are oppositional imperatives, does not change one iota to the fact that this is the thinking of an intellectual, that is, of someone who is there to derive prescriptions. What seems to me so strong in Kant's position, of course, as well as in Lévinas's, is that they reject in principle such a derivation or such a deduction.

JLT: Could not one say, though, that there is in Kant the postulate of "another world"? Let me explain: for prescription to exist, how can one avoid appealing to the fiction of a "counterpart of the real"? In the real, I do not see that there are prescriptions. The real is not prescriptive. Where do prescriptions "come from," then, since one does run into them?

JFL: Postulates in Kant, especially those that deal with the immortality of the soul and with God, have no other function than to give, or return, hope to virtue. No more. They are only postulates and they are not at all necessary to the existence of prescriptions. The "you must" is an obligation that ultimately is not even directly experienced. Because experience by itself always supposes its description, and thus the privilege granted to the play of the descriptive. And so the "you must" is something that exceeds all experience.

JLT: If it exceeds all experience, is it not legitimate to say that the "you must" rests on a metaphysical proposition, namely that experience may be universalizable, that is, that the world may constitute a whole?

JFL: Kant does say that reasonable beings must be able to form a whole that constitutes a sort of suprasensible world. But Kant does not say that the fact of obligation is generated from this. He says merely: "There is the fact of obligation: Act!" And obligation is moral if it takes on the sort of circular relation that is biconditional in the strictly logical sense that action must have with the perspective of a whole of reasonable beings. I say "perspective" but Kant, for his part, uses another word: it is an "Idea." There is an Idea of a suprasensible nature, of a set of human beings, or rather of reasonable beings in general (humans and nonhumans) that can exist together and form a totality. Which is something quite difficult to think through: it is not all an empirical totality, but a practical totality in the Kantian sense, whose members are at once free and obligated. But it is an Idea; it is a sort of horizon that performs a sort of regulatory role with respect to action. That is all.

Now this Idea, what is it? Like all Kantian Ideas, it is simply a pushing to the limit, the maximization of a concept. And the concept here is that of freedom, that is, of reason in its practical use. If one maximizes, everything that is reasonable must be compatible with the action one is carrying out. But this rule of action is not a condition of action. This is very important. It cannot be a condition of action because if it were—and I apologize for these Scholastic minutiae, we would have an imperative that would be hypothetical, as Kant calls it, and such an imperative is of no interest: it belongs to experience; it can be described; it can be derived. So, if you will, I shall answer, since you have put me on Kantian ground: The postulate in question is not a hypothesis on which the existence of imperatives is hung, if I may put it this way. The prescriptive does not hang on the hypothesis of a world of reasonable beings.

JLT: Granted, but this is not what I said, it seems to me. I merely referred to the obligation that the maxim of my action be universalizable. And I was putting forward that, to accept this category of the universalizable, one must admit a "metaphysical" postulate: that the world constitutes a whole.

JFL: No. I think I will continue to disagree with this. It is not a "metaphysical" postulate, and I now use the word "postulate" in a broad sense, as I think you have been. It is not a postulate. To the question, What is it to be just? a supremely Kantian question, I answer: To be just is to act in such a way that (*so daß*, says the German) the maxim of the will may serve as a principle of universal legislation. But the *so daß*, the "in such a way that," what does it mean? It means that it is not a condition that defines justice.

JLT: It is not at all what makes it possible.

JFL: Then the question that remains, and you are quite right to insist on it, is that of this clause. Let us call it a clause, a clause that is theological and negative: "That you may never act in such a way that your action be incompatible with a republic of reasonable beings." This negative clause functions like the idea of negative teleology. The question is whether justice ultimately is: Do whatever ("do whatever" because it is not known what is just) with, as the only regulator of the "whatever," that what you do not be incompatible with a total society of reasonable beings, in the practical sense of the term, that is, that they may themselves be obligated precisely because they are free.

I then ask myself the following: Granted that we have no content for justice, I mean that we have to judge case by case, is justice then to be produced nowhere but in just judgments and never to conform to a prior definition? But the question that remains is: In the "case by case," the one who judges, that is, the subject, the Kantian agent (and also Aristotle's judge, since, after all, this is the fate that Aristotle reserves to his judge, not quite but there are enough similarities), the one who judges, then, can he make do without a finality? Such a finality is not at all a metaphysics, from my point of view. In the Kantian sense, it is not one, it is an Idea. It would be a metaphysics if the finality were presented as a determinant concept. But it is simply one of reason's Ideas. It is a maximization. What Kant is asking is: In the final analysis, what regulates us when we try to judge? Bearing in mind the "fact" that interests the two of us presently, namely, that these judgments are not explainable, that is, derivable, and that neither our instincts nor our interests impel us to judge in a given manner, and having admitted such a "fact," what is it? Not what impels us to judge, but what regulates our judgments.

JLT: What interests me is what impels us to judge and not what regulates our judgments.

JFL: Oh! That is a problem Kant has done away with.

JLT: Let me insist: If, in my view, there are no judgments in the real, why is it that one judges? Why do we make judgments about the real?

JFL: Well, here I don't understand your question. You assert: What interests me is the motivation, the motivation to judge. But that, that is the real. So, within your own problematic, it means that the motivation to judge is part of the real. . . .

JLT: I don't think so. There is nothing in the real that impels me to judge. I would have to suppose that there is a "counterpart of the real" to separate myself from it and to decide.

JFL: There is what Kant says, that there is pleasure and pain, as Freud also says. This is what impels us to judge. If one remains at the level of description, this is what one will find as conditions. It is true that that makes one judge. Freud says so in the *Verneinung*; Kant states it at length in the *Practical Reason* and in the *Critique of Judgment*. You cannot say that in reality nothing impels us to judge. There is pleasure and there is pain, that is, there is a natural finality in desire, or in the *conatus*, or in the persistence of being what one is. There is a finality, that is, there is a rule of judgment. And it is a natural one. This is what one must say when one looks at it from the point of view of description.

JLT: Even if I am judging under the effect of desire or of pain, it still means at least, in this case as well, that I grant or deny value to such and such a thing. And I still do not see that there is such a possibility within the real; I mean by this, that the judgment that I make of the real be immanent to it.

JFL: Well, perhaps it is because you have adopted now an extreme Stoic position which was defended in the third century by a philosopher called Ariston, and which is that of the *adiaphorai*: complete indifferentism. This is an extreme position insofar as it holds that there is no difference in the real between what pleases me and what displeases me, between what makes one preferable over the other. If one takes the point of view of the real, between the fact that my leg gets broken and that a stick gets broken, there is no difference, and therefore no preference to grant to one or the other.

JLT: But in the real, that is not so.

JFL: I think, though, that a position of this sort presupposes that there actually exists a point of view in which one can set oneself up as a perfect describer, and from which the difference between a stick and a leg has no relevance. This point of view is the one the Stoics called the point of view of the All. But it so happens, J. L., that no one occupies the position in question. It is only by an incredible fatuity that one can say "it matters little to me about the leg or the stick." It is not true. I mean that this position can be occupied only at the cost of an extraordinary denial. It requires the denial of the fact that the one who describes "reality" is himself positioned as addressee or hero in a narrative (his "phantasm" as Freud would say) that distributes his pleasures and his pains. It implies further that the game of description can be made equivalent to all the other language games (which is true, thanks to the citation operator) and to all of their pragmatics (which is untrue, because of the same operator). That this position may be a sort of ideal, this is another matter. But I just do not see why a description of reality from the privileged point of view of "exclusive and exhaustive description" should be called "the point of view of the real." It seems to me as unreal as any other. Besides descriptives, there are notably prescriptives. The question is that of their justification. The justification constantly advanced in the ethics and in the beginnings of the treatises of ethics, in critiques, and even in treatises of politics, in the West, is that the compulsion to judge proceeds simply either from desire or from the faculty of pleasure and pain.

JLT: I recognize the difficulties in the position I am defending, difficulties whose nature you underline by the reference to Ariston. It is for that reason that I qualified as "metaphysical" the postulate that it seemed to me one had to admit. My trouble still lies in the fact that I wonder whether it can be avoided.

JFL: I actually think that the question of the "why," in the strict sense of the term never really gets answered. One "notes" (I put quotation marks because the "fact" noted is a "fact of reason"). This is why I made reference to Kant's Ideas earlier: because one "notes," one asseverates, that there are prescriptions. It is a specific language game, the constative one. This language game has no origin; it is not derivable. There you are. This implies that the task is one of multiplying and refining language games. I mean that, ultimately, what does this thesis lead to? To a literature, in the best sense of the term, as an enterprise of experimentation on language games, to a general literature if one can put it this way.

JLT: Very good. It must be understood that prescriptions are a language game like any other, just as there are descriptive language games.

JFL: I hasten to formulate a reservation about this.

JLT: I did not express myself well. Go ahead, state your reservation. . . .

JFL: Yes, I immediately formulate a reservation about what you were saying because in order to say "just as" or "by the same token as," one would have to have a common measure for these different games.

JLT: But to say there is no common measure between the prescriptive and the descriptive games, to oppose them by showing that the first is not derivable from the second, doesn't that lead you to restore the old dualist position?

JFL: No, because there are many games. For example, I absolutely cannot put on the same plane a language game that consists in the description of a reality, let us say, the game of scientific denotation (a "reality," we do not know what that means, but the scientist manages to make herself understood), yes, there is no common measure between such a game and, let us say, an "artistic" language game, quite difficult to define, by the way, and of an experimental sort. Let us say Joyce, in literature. There is no common measure. It is a matter of treatments, I would almost say "tortures," inflicted upon language, but tortures that are natural, by which I mean that they are fundamentally possible in language, in languages. Not simply inflicted upon language, if by the latter we mean, as we tend to since Saussure, semantics and syntax, but inflicted upon the pragmatics of speech [*parole*] as well. This is very important. When you state the formula of water is H_2O you position your addressee, you position yourself as well as your referent, in a way that has no relation to the pragmatics implied in a Joycean proposition.

JLT: Absolutely no relation.

JFL: And so we have no common measure here.

JLT: Yes, but I wonder if by stressing the absence of a common measure between the Joycean game and the didactic game, you do not run the risk of effacing the far more incommensurable specificity of prescriptive language games.

JFL: On the contrary, stressing it is what allows me to situate it correctly. There is no common measure either, between a prescription and a scientific descriptive proposition or a poetic descriptive proposition.

JLT: Yes, but let me explain: since they all stray from a common measure, they are by that fact all rendered uniform, and I am afraid that the strangeness of prescriptives may disappear.

JFL: Not at all. When I say: There is no common measure, it means that we know of nothing in common with these different language games. We merely know that there are several of them, probably not an infinite number, but we really do not know. In any case, the number is not countable for the time being, or if it is, it is so provisionally at best. We also know that these are games that we can enter into but not to play them; they are games that make us into their players, and we know therefore that we are ourselves several beings (by "beings" is meant here proper names that are positioned on the slots of the pragmatics of each of these games). We are the addressees of obligations; we are the senders of artistic messages; and so on. There are many others. My entities are rather large, probably too large. In this way, these games are not at all made equal. On the contrary, they are in a striking disparity. The fact that I myself speak of this plurality does not imply that I am presenting myself as the occupant of a unitary vantage point upon the whole set of these games, but simply that these games have the capacity of talking about themselves. And this is what they are presently doing. Some of them, at least.

JLT: Yes, but I think that some of them, namely, the prescriptive language games, are, from the point of view of their effects, quite singular, quite different from other language games. They have this extraordinary effect of making us change worlds or of changing the world. To change the world in which we live and make us change language games instantly as well. An effect not to be found anywhere else.

JFL: Oh, but I think that it is found elsewhere. It is just that it is different. There are several ways of changing the world. Prescriptions are not alone in causing the world to change. When a scientist describes something that no one has ever seen, the description may pass for purely fictional, and it is in a way, since the reality meant by the discourse will come into being only if names are attached to effects, and these effects exist only inasmuch as new discourses can be grafted onto them. Well, this too changes the world. I mean that a description can change the world. It changes it in another way, to other rhythms, but it changes it no less than a prescription. And when you say, "to change worlds," that means "to change pragmatic positions." There are many ways of changing positions, of changing the pragmatic positions, and these ways define a language game. Every langauge game is bound to a specific pragmatics. And if there are specific pragmatics, it means that a statement, with its form and in the context in which it is uttered, necessarily has an effect upon the world, whatever it may be. A dream, for example: it is a language game that Freud has described fairly well, with its own logic or its own rhetoric. It is a statement that places the utterer in the position of an unknown utterer and the addressee as the ordinary utterer of wakeful discourses, that is, as the dreamer himself. It is an unbelievable transformation of the world, isn't it? And I am not even talking about what happens with respect to the reference of the dream, which is something else, even more astonishing, certainly. I don't think that there is any discourse without efficacy. The efficacy of prescriptives, though, is singular; it resembles no other, to be sure. What distinguishes them from other statements is the fact that they include explicitly, in their form, the expectation of their own efficacy. Even if the prescriptive is not followed by an effect, in the usual sense, it is nonetheless the case that its recipient finds himself in a state of obligation, the obligation to reply, or not to reply, to do as he wills, but still he is in a state of obligation. It is "prior" to the reply, and even "prior" to the understanding of its content.

JLT: You said that the perspective that is opening up is that of a general literature. Let us return now, if you will, to the pragmatics of Judaism.

JFL: God commands. One does not know very well what he commands. He commands obedience, that is, that one place oneself in the position of the pragmatic genre of obligation. Then he commands a whole slew of small, unbelievable things: how to cook lamb, and so on. Which is surprising, because one does not expect God to hand out kitchen recipes, and it takes the Jewish people by surprise also. What is proper to Judaism is to say: Well, God himself we know nothing about; there is nothing to say about it. We call that God, but ultimately we do not know what we are saying when we say God. We know nothing about it. We merely say: There is a law. And when we say "law," it does not mean that the law is defined and that it suffices to abide by it. There is a law, but we do not know what this law says. There is a kind of a law of laws, there is a metalaw that says: "Be just." That is all that matters in Judaism: "Be just." But we do not know what it is to be just. That is, we have to be "just." It is not "Abide by this"; it is not "Love one another," etc. All of that is child's play. "Be just"; case by case, every time it will be necessary to decide, to commit oneself, to judge, and then to meditate if that was just. It implies that this community thinks the problem of the prescriptive in terms of the future. The discourse that is implied in this language game is, in my view, a discourse about history. I mean "history" in a precise sense: what is to be done. That is all that is important. It is a game of the history of the human community inasmuch as it is held by prescriptions, and only by that. As far as being, and hypotheses about being, are concerned, all of this is without interest. Lévinas is categorical on this, and I think he is quite right.

JLT: Are you saying that Judaism rejects ontology?

JFL: It is quite clear that if there is a question that Judaism refuses, it is that of ontology. I would say that it is inherent to oppression to import into a language game a question that comes from another one and to impose it. I do not know; it is the same thing with American Indians. It is quite obvious: they play a language game that is common to a great many peoples, the narrative game. It is a very big game with many things in it, but it still is a type of language game. To raise constantly the question of being with respect to all language games, to reduce the language games to ontology, is to attempt to carry out the whole Hegelian operation all over again, that is, it is to take each of the games for a figure of the spirit and to show that within each of these figures, or each of these formations, the spirit is always asking itself the question of the real. And then one would go on to hierarchize them in order to show that one dominates another because it overcomes it or sublates it. This is quite obvious in a reading of Hegel's texts on the Jews, the so-called early writings; the functioning of the operation is quite apparent. And one can see very easily how it can legitimize oppression. It becomes obvious that there is a congruence between the domination of ontology and the torture inflicted to language games that are not those of ontological discourse.

JLT: Yes, because at that moment, it is supposed that the so-called ontological language game can translate all the others.

JFL: Yes, that is right. And the problem is indeed one of translation and translatability. It so happens that languages are translatable, otherwise they are not languages; but language games are not translatable, because, if they were, they would not be language games. It is as if one wanted to translate the rules and strategies of chess into those of checkers.

JLT: You are saying then that ontology is a specific kind of language game. There is thus the Parmenides game, if it is true that he was the first to play it.

JFL: Yes, just as there is, on the opposite side, the Moses game. And there are many others. One can verify this multiplicity of the position of the addressee. When one says "language game," one must always admit that this game is played with someone; I mean there always is an addressee. And to this addressee, one addresses all sorts of discourses. And in each instance, one is in a game, a game with rules, and I play with these rules in order to achieve some effects upon the one I am playing with.

JLT: So, for you, there are no statements that one separates out, that is, that one could extract from the tactical game that is being played between two or three players.

JFL: Quite right.

JLT: And so as general and trivial an utterance as "that's life!" you won't dissociate it from its communicational situation?

JFL: I would rather say, from its "pragmatic context," that is, from the type of game that is being played. And, of course, it is very complicated, because one can play simultaneously several games; in fact, this is nearly always the case. One goes from one game to another. It is very rare for us to play a homogeneous game with a given partner for a set period of time. It is more often the case that one jumps from one game to another, and that one statement must be referred back to the game it belongs to, whereas the very next statement must be referred to another. Nonetheless, in principle the statement is always determinable, by means of the nature of the forms of the statements and by their own efficiencies.

JLT: Well then, this game can be played with the texts that you have published. When you have written: We ought to be pagan and just, one can refuse to separate this statement from the pragmatic context in which it appears, and one can further refuse to treat it as a thesis. On the contrary, one can think that this is a move, a move you have played on a given page for a given period of time. Is that the case? It is, in any case, quite unlikely.

JFL: No, on the contrary, I think it is very likely. In fact, it seems to me to be quite the case. And only the case. I do not think I have ever written a line that did not have this function. The least of these statements must be understood as a move in a context; in this fashion, everything I may have written is always tactical, that is, it always takes into account the context in which it appears. And a statement has no other function; it always has an extremely modest scope. It is in this sense that I do not believe myself to be a philosopher, in the proper sense of the term, but a "politician." But this term remains to be defined; the meaning of the word "politician" must be completely overhauled. And such an overhauling would consist in thinking of all discourses as moves in language games. You see?

JLT: If the statement I referred to earlier, that appears in *Instructions païennes* [*Pagan Instructions*], is to be taken as you have just said, in its pragmatic context, and if it cannot be taken from this context without being altered, then it is no longer a slogan. Then why *Instructions païennes*? Why draw up instructions whose validity is limited to one move? They can no longer be called "instructions," I should think. They could be called reveries, remarks, opinions, but not instructions. An instruction requires that anyone who reads the proposition it is contained in, can make it his or her own. Once again, it must be thought that it is universalizable for any and every pragmatic context, that is, for any and every move.

JFL: Your example suits me very well because *Instructions païennes* is probably the book in which the aspect "pragmatic move" is most apparent. The context is that of the situation of the French intelligentsia at more or less the time of the elections of 1978. And the pragmatic context is explicit, something that is not always the case in everything I have concocted. If one were to look for the pragmatic context of *Discours, figure* [*Discourse, Figure*], for example, it would not be as readily apparent, even though it is decisive. But to say that a given statement in this little book, in *Instructions païennes*, presents itself as an instruction and that, under these conditions, because there is instruction, the latter must have a sort of universal scope, that, I do not think can be said, because an instruction is not a slogan, quite the contrary, as you yourself have said. There are no slogans in *Instructions païennes*. An instruction is precisely an indication of what is appropriate to do in a specific pragmatic context. For example, the instructions may be those of a military commander to his subordinates in a given situation, or those of a school superintendent to her teaching staff. They are always local. If the context disappears, the instructions no longer have any meaning. They are not slogans, then. A slogan belongs to a general strategy. And a general strategy presupposes a permanent context; slogans can be turned into specific instructions in accordance with circumstances. When one speaks of instructions, one is basically implying that one does not really know the permanent general context and that one would have to be quite conceited to be able to do an analysis of it.

And so one works almost "case by case," move by move, and instructions are a move-by-move process. It is like the "instructions to the user" on a sack of cement. It is on that level.

JLT: It is universal.

JFL: It is universal only inasmuch as one has a sack of cement in front of oneself and it is to be used in the stated manner. Otherwise these instructions on how to use the cement of an absent sack, or any other, are of no interest. They lose all value of efficiency as instructions.

JLT: I have the feeling that the misunderstanding stems perhaps from an error on my part, because you are speaking of a pragmatic context and I think I am hearing "conjuncture," and, in such a case, I understand very well what you mean. It is indeed the political in the classical sense of the term. There is a conjuncture, and then one issues directives, instructions that are valid as long as the conjuncture lasts and does not change. Is that it?

JFL: What is the alternative here?

JLT: I understand "pragmatic context" in the strict sense, namely as the effect produced by a text, that exists only in a given text for the one who reads it and will not even be reproduced in another text.

JFL: Yes, but both come together in a book like *Instructions païennes*. [That they do] is probably one of its properties. On the one hand, what is talked about in the book is the political context, let us put it this way, which is something else than political though, because, insofar as it is a question of showing to what extent the great Marxist narrative is no longer able to mobilize French intellectuals, it exceeds a little the analysis of political forces in the traditional sense of the term, the established, institutionalized political forces.

JLT: In short, it is the conjuncture "of the intellectuals."

JFL: It is a conjuncture. All right. And it does indeed have to do with the politics of the intelligentsia. This is something that is described in the book. On the other hand, the book implicates itself in this description, that is, it takes its place in it and develops a pragmatics which is its own, and which is that of a dialogue, since we have to go through the forms at this point. A somewhat odd pragmatics.

This form of the dialogue deserves some of our attention. It is not exactly a Platonic dialogue; it is rather a "dialogue" in the sense of the eighteenth century. And this form of dialogue must have some efficacy on the reader, I should think. What is the position of, and how is positioned, the addressee to whom one is transmitting neither a treatise nor a series of slogans but reflections bearing on the context in which he finds himself as well as the utterer of the dialogue? You see. This is where I am playing a little on the word "instructions," taking it in its double meaning: "instruction" means "local and temporary prescription" with no universal value, and thus it is a hypothetical imperative, if there are imperatives; "instruction" also means that one reads a dialogue to get instructed, which is something that is connoted by the old tradition that comes from Platonism – a dialogue sets a stage between two individuals where one knows more than the other, or a stage where someone knows more than he knows himself to know, always with a built-in inequality. This is the case, by the way, in *Instructions païennes*. It is likely that the reader of this dialogue finds himself or herself in the position of addressee, actually of second meta-addressee, of the more learned of the two characters who are dialoguing. In this sense, s/he is giving himself or herself instruction. So, you see, if one looks for the pragmatics of the book, this will have to be the direction one will have to explore. But I do not see what possible objection you could raise against this. The pragmatics is inscribed in the context, and the context itself is taken as a reference of the discourse of the book. There is mutual inclusion here. It seems to me that this is a frequent enough status for books: they position their reference and, at the same time, they are themselves part of the type of "reality" that they position. And their efficacy comes from that.

JLT: Yes, this situation is indeed the most common, but with this clause: authors do not usually reserve for themselves the position you seem to want for yourself, namely, that it is not possible to extract any statements out of the books that you write, to let them stand by themselves, and to turn them into slogans. Otherwise, what must one think about theses such as "we must be pagan; we must march toward paganism?" Surely they are directives.

JFL: Yes. That is absolutely true. The book says: Here is how one must proceed. Well, where is the objection?

JLT: Generally, those who write this type of book and make this type of assertion acknowledge that they are issuing prescriptions.

JFL: Yes, but careful here! In terms of the opposition that is to be found already in Parmenides, and then is reiterated in Plato and especially in Aristotle, it is one thing to say: This is my opinion, and another to say: This is true. In our case, I do not wish to make use of this difference because it still is a matter of prescription under the form of instructions, even if they are temporary, whereas opinion is not prescriptive in itself in Aristotle's problematics. But let us take, if you will, the difference between a concept and an Idea in the Kantian problematic. The paganism elaborated in the Instructions in question is more akin to an Idea in Kant's sense. This paganism is not demonstrated; it is not derived; it cannot be articulated or deduced. It is simply the Idea of a society, that is, ultimately, of a set of diverse pragmatics (a set that is neither totalizable nor countable, actually). The specific feature of this set would be that the different language games that are caught up in this pagan universe are incommunicable to each other. They cannot be synthesized into a unifying metadiscourse. All that can be done is to give them a proper name, and when I say "pagan," that is what the word "means." It is not a slogan; it is rather a denomination, you see. An appellation for a social universe, since this is what we are talking about. A field for the emitting and transmitting of messages that deal with realities. Messages regulated by different types of "compass," and thus positioning several ways of turning reality out. This social universe is formed by a plurality of games without any one of them being able to claim that it can say all the others. I don't say it either, because when I say: This here, this is paganism, it is simply onomastics.

The project falls within what Kant called an "Idea" since the social universe is undemonstrable or antinomic, and it is presented as such and proposed as such. There is always present in the idea of the "Idea" in Kant, this notion of the maximization of the concept: one follows the concept beyond what reality can give it as sensible to subsume and one sees then what can be thought by extending thus the scope of the concept. The Idea of paganism functions like that perhaps, all things being equal . . . .

JLT: But your text does not function just like that. The way you speak of it, one could think of it as being merely a description. Let us say that it is a denomination, a name that you are giving to an uncounted set of games, among which no game would be privileged. But you also say: One ought to be pagan. This is a prescription.

JFL: You make the following observation: One cannot merely say that I give a description of the multiplicity of language games in their incommunicability; I also give out instructions, that is, I prescribe something. This is entirely true. *Instructions païennes*, as its name indicates, is a compound of several language games, that of dialogue, as I have said, but also that of the prescriptions contained in the dialogue that are addressed to an addressee who is one of the two dialogists, and addressed as well, over and above him, to the reader as well. The fact that I say "one ought . . ." is not bothersome per se. In *Instructions païennes* there are indeed some prescriptives. I do not see what the trouble is.

JLT: The trouble is in this question: How can there be prescriptives in the pagan?

JFL: But of course there can be! There are prescriptives in the pagan! It is fundamental, even. Just as there is a politics in the Greek city, just as there are decisions to be made by Aristotle's judge, just as the sage has to decide whether to be a father or not, to fall in love or not, and so on. There always are prescriptions; one cannot live without prescriptions. It was Ariston's error to have claimed the opposite. I believe that one of the properties of paganism is to leave prescriptions hanging, that is, they are not derived from an ontology. This seems essential to me.

I would like to add one thing. In this matter of instruction, though I start from a description, I do not draw prescriptions from it because one cannot derive prescriptions from descriptions. I start with a description, and what one can do with a description—and that is why I was using the Kantian term of "Idea" a little while ago—is to extend, or maximize, as much as possible what one believes to be contained in the description. There is, then, a language game that bears upon the description of the context of the French intelligentsia today, especially as a result of the fact that the great narratives that it used to dedicate itself to, no longer can claim its allegiance or even concern. And the idea that emerges is that there is a multiplicity of small narratives. And from that, "one ought to be pagan" means "one must maximize as much as possible the multiplication of small narratives." This "ought" belongs to the game of dialectics in the Kantian sense, in which there is the use of the concept that is not a use of knowledge but a use of the Idea. You see. I would distinguish then, if you will, between prescriptions that the reader can receive as they are, and that the provincial of the *Instructions païennes* receives from the foreigner, the wog, and an "ought" that the reader receives properly, the "ought" of ideal maximization that says: And if we pushed to the end this idea of a multiplication of language games? Now, this "ought" does not signal that a field of prescriptions is opening up; it marks a transit point from a descriptive game whose goal is knowledge of the given, to a descriptive game (by Ideas) of the exploration of the possible. The transit point is marked by the prescriptive.

Fourth Day
A Casuistry of the Imagination

JLT: All that you have said concerns me a great deal because one is led to think that what you call paganism is a sort of satire, in the Latin sense of the word, namely, that all the known language games are maintained. If none is privileged, none is dropped either. We keep the prescriptive game; we keep the narrative game. Then, where does the specificity of paganism lie? And a further question: At what point does one decide to change games?

JFL: First question: What makes paganism? It consists in the fact that each game is played as such, which implies that it does not give itself as the game of all the other games or as the true one. This is why the other day I was saying that I was betraying Lévinas because it is obvious that the very way in which I take over his doctrine or his theory, or his description of the prescriptive, is alien to his own. In his view, it is the transcendental character of the other in the prescriptive relation, in the pragmatics of prescription, that is, in the (barely) lived experience of obligation, that is truth itself. This "truth" is not ontological truth, it is ethical. But it is a truth in Lévinas's own terms. Whereas for me, it cannot be the truth. There is as much truth in a narrative even if it can lead to the worst "errors," as in mythologies, for example, if they are errors, which I do not believe they are. There are "risks" in narrations; there are also risks in prescriptions. It is not a matter of privileging a language game above others. That would be something like saying: The only important game, the only true one, is chess. That is absurd. What is pagan is the acceptance of the fact that one can play several games, and that each of these games is interesting in itself insofar as the interesting thing is to play moves. And to play moves means precisely to develop ruses, to set the imagination to work.

Now when you ask me, Why do you pass from one game to another? I reply that it does not worry me very much. If we need a name for the "cause," let us call it the will. . . . If one is pagan, it is certainly not because one thinks that one game is better than another; it is because one has several kinds of games at one's disposal. There are even some that are not invented yet and that one could invent by instituting new rules; and that is quite interesting. It is in this way that something like the imagination, or the will, I do not know, could develop. And when I say "develop," I do not mean it in the sense of a progress; I mean the fact that one can introduce into the pragmatics, into our relations with others, forms of language that are at the same time unexpected and unheard of, as forms of efficacy. Either because one has made up new moves in an old game or because one has made up a new game.

JLT: Yes, but I have the feeling, then, that it is a cinch to be pagan, and that many people are pagans and do not know it. An artist, someone who practices the "art" game, who paints a painting, or makes a movie, can also be someone who practices the game of justice, it seems to me.

JFL: But of course. What you are saying is both true and false, I think. It is true to the extent that most people, except if they are quite bizarre, to call it that, have at their disposal the existing multiplicity of language games, and it is true that an artist is at the same time someone who has to decide if she is going to sue for a divorce or not. In that sense, there are, of course, prescriptions to assume, obligations to feel, and decisions to take. Very good. But there is also the fact, and this is where what you are saying is not true, that very often, for many of us, probably for most of us, when we play some of these games, we play them without inventiveness. That is, we do not play any "master strokes." I think that pagans are artists, that is, they can move from one game to another, and in each of these games (in the optimal situation) they try to figure out new moves. And even better, they try to invent new games. What we call an "artist" in the usual sense of the term, is someone who, in relation to a given purport, the purport of the canvas and the medium of the *picta*, for example, proposes new rules of the painting game. Same thing for the so-called independent cinema, or for music.

The question then is whether it is possible to achieve the same level of refinement, if I may call it that, and the same power, in several games. And this, without privileging any of them, without saying: This is the good one. This is what paganism would be. The point is not that one keeps the games, but that, in each of the existing games, one effects new moves, one opens up the possibility of new efficacies in the games with their present rules. And, in addition, one changes the rules: one can play a given game with other rules, and when one changes the rules, one has changed the game, because a game is primarily defined by its rules. And here again, it is a problem of inventiveness in language games. When Parmenides begins to reflect upon being, he does introduce a new language game (I am deliberately simplifying) that had not been played until then. A very complicated game, a very refined one, very difficult and apparently most amusing. There! Same thing for Freud. We are getting back to proper names; each one of them is a name borne by a game, and it is the artists that always establish the rules of a language game that did not exist before. That is how there is paganism. A sign that people are not pagan as they should be is that they believe in the signified of what they are saying, that they stick to this signified, and that they think that they are in the true. This is where paganism stops and where something like doctrine, let us say, gets back in. Whereas one should be able to have, in relation to what one invents in language games, a properly pagan attitude, an attitude that I will not call skeptical because the word has been much abused, but, let us say, libertine or libertarian.

JLT: If I follow you, it is not enough to keep the old games but one should refine them and modify them; one should further introduce new ways of playing already known games. And for every game that one practices, even the game of justice, variations come by way of the imagination. What I do not see very well is what sort of modifiction one can bring to the rules of the game of justice. It seems to me to be extremely crude. It is true that we can sophisticate the Parmenides game easily, but the "do this, do that" game, I find very limited.

JFL: Oh, but it gets sophisticated by itself. For the sake of the argument, let us remain in the field of prescriptives since we admit in principle that the game of justice is played in this field. Well, if you compare the actual prescriptions in effect in the eighteenth century in Europe with those of today, you can see that the sophistication today is very great. Very few of the old prescriptions survive, and today there are new ones, quite surprising and not at all dependent on the old ones, about such things as hospitality, solidarity, and so on. It is very easy to see this.

JLT: But there is a prescription that resists in spite of everything, precisely because of its crude state: "Thou shalt not kill!" for example.

JFL: But the prescription "thou shalt not kill" has always been festooned with exceptions, and all these exceptions have implied "thou shalt kill." It was "thou shalt kill" under certain conditions. And the conditions ultimately determined the subject that gives the order, that is, the utterer of the prescription. This is a very large issue since it is the issue of authority. Who has authority to kill? It is obvious that it is not at all the same authority in the thirteenth and in the twentieth century. One could say that there is a great sophistication in the authorization of killing if one is sensitive to its variations from one century to another, because the wars and the massacres of the sixteenth century are one thing; the authority to kill in what is called "terrorism" in general, which is a rather modern phenomenon as terrorism and not as violence, is something else altogether. It is quite clear that there is a great sophistication even as far as what this precept, "thou shalt not kill," admits as exception, and it is considerable.

JLT: Your remark had to do with exceptions to the prescription. Even if today the jurisprudence of murder is not what it was in the Middle Ages, there still remains at bottom the "thou shalt not kill" that does not vary, it seems to me.

JFL: I do not share your view. "Thou shalt not kill" is for us a Christian prescription, even if it is not only Christian. Jews take a much more nuanced position on this subject. It is rare for them to issue categorical prescriptions, except for "listen!" Generally, their prescriptions are circumstantial. And there are cases in which one can kill.

JLT: We are still in the area of exceptions.

JFL: If one examines Judaic practice, one can see that it admits that one can kill in some cases: to reestablish justice, in point of fact.

JLT: Christians admit to this as well.

JFL: Christians are hesitant about this. They are rather the ones who present the authorization to kill as an exception to the basic law because Christianity ought to exclude all violence and there should be no exceptions. If there is a law of love, it ought to be absolute. There is actually a Christian tendency in this direction. But in practice, it is not the case, and, as we all know, they have often killed.

But, if you will, I would say that for them "thou shalt not kill" remains a sort of horizon. It is a prescriptive that, by virtue of the fact
that it is categorical, forms the general horizon of this civilization.
And that survives through the idea of Enlightenment under the name
of "Project for a Perpetual Peace," for example, where it is a matter
of eliminating the occasions of killing or the "justifications" for
killing.

JLT: But independently of the problem of exceptions, there remains the fact of a general law of justice, and this law is basic, as you
say, because it is justified by a foundational metaphysical discourse.

JFL: Yes, the canonical Christian narrative . . . from which the
law of love and the "thou shalt not kill" are derived. The poverty in
sophistication that makes you apprehensive comes from this very
metaphysical overlay. What I find striking about the prescriptions of
Judaism is that, in principle, there never is any such discourse: the
law is presented as making for obligation, but it is not justified. At
bottom one does not know who is speaking, and one does not know
why what is said is said. When Abraham hears that he has to sacrifice
Isaac, he sets out to do it, but he does not say, "it is for my good,"
or "it is for the good of Israel. . . ."

JLT: Where is the sophistication in such a case?

JFL: I mean that, in this case, the case of Judaism, the language
game of prescription is kept in its purity; it is not taken over by
ontological discourse, and it is only if this game is kept pure that it
can really be sophisticated, to use this term again. Of course, my
example of Judaism may seem somewhat forced; after all, there is a
whole religion, an entire set of beliefs, that rest upon this pure prescriptive. But what I mean is that between this (actually Lévinasian)
conception of prescription and the conception of a given Sophist, or
even Aristotle's conception of prescriptives in matters of ethics or
politics, there is not much difference. In both instances, though in
different fashion, there is the same thought, namely, that prescriptives
cannot be justified; they cannot be made into the conclusions of a
reasoning; there is no description and no definition of the prescribing
authority. What has been called the conventionalism of the Sophists
was probably not conventionalism, but rather an awareness of the
fact that not only are laws given, but that there must be laws. There
is a language game called "command" and "be obligated," and one
must play it. But who is authorized to issue laws, is a question that
must be left hanging. And even when the subject who is authorized
to command is defined, the question why he commands what he

does, is even more complicated. In other words, there is, I think, in the position of the Sophists, or at least among some of them, the same humor in relation to commands as in an entire Jewish tradition. I say "humor" and I choose the word carefully. I think that it is this humor that allows for refinement in matters of prescription. It seems to me that it is the Hassidim, or a thought like theirs, that first reached the maximum of refinement. One does not find there all the massive character of commands, but, on the contrary, the effort to become ever more sensitive to the strange property that a statement of command is a statement that cannot be deduced. And it is only at the cost of such a sensitivization that one will slowly realize that what is important in this language game is obligation as a pragmatic relation and not as content.

JLT: That raises the question of an unjust obligation, the obligation that being overrefined ends up being unjust.

JFL: Yes.

JLT: How do you conceive of it? When is one unjust?

JFL: But it is just this, the pressure of this question, that is implied by the idea of refinement in relation to obligation, since we do not have a rule for justice. That is, to be just is not a matter of conforming to laws. Conformity is an idea of justice that is akin to *mimèsis*, which comes from Platonism and the entire ontological tradition, since it can only be stated in ontological discourse. There is a nature of being and it suffices, if I may put it this way, to conform to it in order to be just. Whereas in the tradition of the prescriptives that I call "just," and that constitutes the game of justice, there is no ontology, and so it does not suffice to conform to be just. And everybody in the Jewish tradition knows that those who conform the most can be perfectly unjust, and those that conform the least, perfectly just. Both obtain. Caught up in a pragmatic situation of obligation, we have no rules of conduct. And to be just is to venture to formulate a hypothesis on what is to be done, and that is where one gets back to this idea of "Idea." One regulates oneself upon the imagining of effects, upon a sort of finality. It is the imagining of the effects of what one will decide that will guide the judgment. It is the end, thus, the idea of the effect, that commands, that functions as "cause."

JLT: Allow me to ask again, what is it to be unjust?

JFL: To be unjust?

JLT: If I hear a rabbi tell me "throw this flower pot out of the window!" a debate begins to take place then. Am I just if I obey? Or, on the contrary, am I perhaps unjust if I hurl the flower pot out of the window?

JFL: Absolutely. It is an excellent example because the refinement that Judaism brings to the notion of obligation is precisely that one has to watch out for prescriptions that appear to be just or authorized; they are not always to be taken literally, and they may result in the most extreme injustice. They must be taken as much as traps as obligatory prescriptions. And thus they always refer one back to responsibility, to the responsibility of listening, of lending oneself to obligation. And what does the latter mean?

No one can say what the being of justice is. That, at least, seems certain. The rabbi cannot tell either. When the rabbi issues the command, think that, at the moment that he is speaking ("at the moment that he is speaking": we are back in instructions), that is what is to be done. One can suppose that because the rabbi is honest, because he is just, because he is as just as one can hope to be, one can suppose that if he tells you that, it is not in order to deceive you. But one cannot be sure. Even if he is not seeking to deceive you, he himself may be deceived. Here we are in a relation that is proper to prescriptives, because there is no test for the just whereas there is for the true. One cannot compare what the rabbi says with a state of affairs (a *Sachverhalt*). There is no state of affairs that corresponds to what the rabbi says, and it is proper to prescriptives not to make commensurate their discourse with a reality, since the "reality" they speak of is still to be. What Judaism, and especially the Hassidim, and some Sophists as well, teach us, is how to be suspicious of prescriptions. Ontology, on the other hand, teaches us not to be suspicious. With the ontological axe, one always cuts a divide between that which conforms to being and that which does not, by calling "just" that which does. But it is obvious that this is untenable, and modernity knows it.

JLT: Let us take a look at it differently, if you will. What do we do with a thesis like "it is unjust; I rebel"? How is one to say this if one does not know what is just and what is unjust? If the determination of the just is the object of a perpetual sophistic debate? And yet, in everyday life, everybody says, "It is unjust." And generally such a judgment leads, by no means always, but often enough, to rebellion.

JFL: Absolute injustice would occur if the pragmatics of obligation, that is, the possibility of continuing to play the game of the just, were excluded. That is what is unjust. Not the opposite of the just, but that which prohibits that the question of the just and the unjust be, and remain, raised. Thus, obviously, all terror, annihilation, massacre, etc., or their threat, are, by definition, unjust. The people whom one massacres will no longer be able to play the game of the just and the unjust. But moreover, any decision that takes away, or in which it happens that one takes away, from one's partner in a current pragmatics, the possibility of playing or replaying a pragmatics of obligation—a decision that has such an effect is necessarily unjust. But of course one must imagine this effect, these effects. . . .

JLT: It seems to me that this pragmatic analysis could be extended to a certain type of "terrorism."

JFL: What is being called "terrorism" is something that actually includes two types of operations. There is a type of violence that, at bottom, belongs to the game of war: I am in front of an adversary, I make a breakthrough, an incursion; I destroy a part of his forces. I do not see what is objectionable about that. When the group Red Army Fraction makes an incursion and destroys the American computer in Heidelberg, that is war; the group considers itself at war; it is waging war and it is actually destroying a part of the forces of the adversary. Very good: that is part of the rather exact game that is a two-sided war. But when the same group kidnaps Schleyer and blackmails a third party with Schleyer's death as the stake, then we are in an altogether different violence that has no relation to the previous one and which alone, in my view, deserves the name of "terrorism." It is of the same nature whether it is used by the State or by a minority group. And in such a case, it falls within what I was just saying: It excludes the game of the just. It excludes the game of the just because the Schleyer in question is obviously taken as a means here. He is threatened with death, but this threat is addressed to a third party, not to him. The same Schleyer was at risk of being killed in an attack, but that is not the same thing at all. Then he would have been treated like an adversary, and, in any case, he considered himself as being indeed at war; he had himself surrounded by armed bodyguards. So he would be taken as an adversary and destroyed as such. I am not necessarily in favor, mind you, but I am saying that it is war. The taking of hostages is something else; it is the death of another person, a threat of death, that is used as an argument. It is pedagogical politics ("We will make you aware of the collusion between Schleyer and the State's police terror!") that looks pedagogical but cannot really be. It is a politics in which the real aim is to force the third party to yield. And the third party is not just the State, of which one makes oneself the threatening teacher, it is public opinion. One invites public opinion to apply pressure on the State by applying pressure on it through fear.

When the violent group attacks directly someone like Buback or like Ponto, it is a two-sided game; it is war between two groups, between two groupings: on one side, the political-economic rulers, and on the other, a group that thinks that these rulers are unjust and that, since it is not possible to have them become just, they must be destroyed. In itself, this is not monstrous. If one takes things in this fashion, history is replete with thousands of precedents, even among the Jewish people. Those are states of war. We are dealing with two systems of prescriptions that encroach upon each other and that are incompatible. That leads to a war.

JLT: You are saying, two systems of prescriptions. There is [German Chancellor] Schmidt's set of prescriptions and then there is the Red Army Fraction's system of prescriptions?

JFL: That is right.

JLT: And you are saying that, at this point, one is just and the other unjust?

JFL: No. I am saying that they are incompatible. I am not judging.

JLT: You are not judging.

JFL: No, I am describing.

JLT: Yes, but they, they are judging. They say: "It is unjust."

JFL: Yes. They think the other side is unjust.

JLT: Then we can get back to the question: Is that warranted?

JFL: How do you mean, "warranted?"

JLT: Doesn't one have the right to say that?

JFL: But of course one has the right to say that! In any case, they take that right. On both sides, they take it.

JLT: Yes, they take it. But if you do not have any criteria to say that a given thing is just or unjust?

JFL: It goes to show to what extent it is difficult to decide. For example, is it just that there be an American computer in Heidelberg that, among other things, is used to program the bombing of Hanoi? In the final analysis, someone like Schleyer thinks so. In the final analysis, the "Baader-Meinhof" group thinks not. Who is right? It is up to everyone to decide!

JLT: And you think it is unjust that there be an American computer in Heidelberg?

JFL: Yes, absolutely. I can say that such is my opinion. I feel committed in this respect.

JLT: I know that well, but I want us to get back to this. You say: "It is unjust." How can you say it, if you do not have a representation of what justice ought to be, unless you derive this prescription of acting against from something else?

JFL: No. I do not think that it can be derived. I think that one can try to derive it. It can be derived in Kantian fashion; it can be derived in Hegelian fashion; it can be derived in Christian fashion. There is thus a whole slew of possible motifs. I mean "motif" almost in the sense of embroidery.

JLT: It is always derived then?

JFL: Since there are far too many motifs, it is extremely difficult to derive. I mean that, actually, those are the motifs that one can call "ideological." If you asked me why I am on that side, I think that I would answer that I do not have an answer to the question "why?" and that this is of the order of . . . transcendence. That is, here I feel a prescription to oppose a given thing, and I think that it is a just one. This is where I feel that I am indeed playing the game of the just.

JLT: So, at this point, you are describing justice as a transcendence.

JFL: If you will, except that the transcendence is empty.

JLT: The transcendence is empty. I fully agree.

JFL: That is, it does not say what it says, what it prescribes.

JLT: Okay. But there is a transcendence of justice.

JFL: There is a transcendence of justice.

JLT: This is what I wanted you to grant me.

JFL: I fear that there may be a misprision on your part with respect to the term "transcendence." I take it exactly in Lévinas's sense. That is, that there is an obligation that comes, if you will, to me under the form . . .

JLT: . . . of a prescriptive.

JFL: Yes, I feel obligated with respect to the prescription that the Americans should get out of Vietnam, or the French out of Algeria. You see. It does not mean that there is a transcendence. When I say "transcendence," it means: I do not know who is sending me the prescription in question.

JLT: I fully agree. I am not saying that there is a transcendence.

JFL: If I were to be pushed, I would answer that what regulates this feeling of obligation is the Kantian Idea. The Americans in Vietnam, the French in Algeria, were doing something that prohibited that the whole of reasonable beings could continue to exist. In other words, the Vietnamese or the Algerians saw themselves placed in a position where the pragmatics of obligation was forbidden to them. They had the right to rebel.

JLT: I would be surprised, allow me to say, if that were to be the true reason of this choice. I would rather say that one is taken hold of by a prescription that one cannot avoid.

JFL: Oh, one can always avoid it. For my part, I prefer the thesis of pure and simple transcendence, that is, there is a willing. When I say this, I am answering like a pure Kantian. There is a willing. What this will wants, we do not know. We feel it in the form of an obligation, but this obligation is empty, in a way. So if it can be given a content in the specific occasion, this content can be only circumscribed by an Idea. The Idea is the one I just stated, that is, "the whole of reasonable beings" or the preservation of the possibility of the prescriptive game. But this whole of reasonable beings, I do not know if the will wants it or what it wants with it. I will never know it. I do know that, at that moment, in the case of Vietnam or Algeria, to want this whole of reasonable beings effectively leads to the opposition of imperialist actions in Algeria or in Vietnam. And thus eventually to the support of the group that attacks the computer in Heidelberg.

I will repeat: in this case, there is not, for me, any incompability between this regulatory Idea and the transcendental character of the will that guides me on one hand, and the means implemented by the action, on the other. But, in the other case, on the contrary, that is, in the three-sided strategy, the one used with Schleyer or with Aldo Moro, it is the reverse. It is a politics that is absolutely "immoral." You understand what I mean. One is working in a tripartite fashion, and the blow one delivers to the other is not a blow that weakens him. Whether Schleyer is alive or dead changes nothing to the economic direction of Germany; whether Moro is alive or not changes nothing to the political direction of Italy. The blow is not struck on the adversary but it is hoped that the blow will be borne by the third party, the witness, public opinion. In such a case, everyone is caught "without freedom," in a causality of nature. And in matters of obligation, nature is the threat to life. Whereas in a two-sided battle, my opponent thinks that what I think and do is unjust, and I think that what he does and thinks is unjust. Well, his freedom is complete and so is mine. With a hostage, I am applying . . . not even "pressure." It is much more than that. It is the social bond taken as a fact of nature.

JLT: If you will allow me, I will put things in another way. You oppose war to terrorism: that is true, provided that it is specified that modern war, since 1914 at least, is terroristic.

JFL: Of course. It is a necessary qualification. Cf. Ludendorff's *The Total War.*

JLT: I would like to return now to what you were saying about the game of justice. How can you say that it is a language game like the others when it has the distinctive feature of including a transcendence, a finality, an Idea?

JFL: As far as the Idea is concerned, I am not sure that it is the only one. I think that the "artist" game also implies ideas, well an Idea. But here I do not know; you are making me talk beyond what I am capable of articulating.

JLT: In the case of prescriptions, the pragmatics is somewhat peculiar, since one of the elements, one of the points of the pragmatic triangle is transcendental, if I may say so.

JFL: Of course it is peculiar. But listen, I want to underscore something that seems essential to me. When language games are said to be different, it means that, in the pragmatic triangle, to treat things very simply, a given pole will be forgotten, for example, or completely neutralized, taken to be superfluous. For instance, it is not known to whom most speculative discourses are addressed. The pole of the addressee is occulted. In the game of the prescriptive it is the first sender who is occulted. It is not known who obligates; there is nothing to be said about it; it cannot be brought over to the narrative pole or to the referent.

When I say "transcendence," I take over a term used by Lévinas, and also by Kant when the latter says that that which obligates is something absolutely beyond our intelligence. In terms of language games, it must be granted that to understand what a prescription or an obligation is, the pole of the sender must be neutralized. Only if it is neutralized, will one become sensitive, not to what it is, not to the reason why it says what it says, not even to what it says, but to the fact that it prescribes or obligates. It may seem paradoxical, but there is nothing paradoxical about it. It is only in relation to our conception of language games that it is paradoxical. For us, a langauge is first and foremost someone talking. But there are langauge games in which the important thing is to listen, in which the rule deals with audition. Such a game is the game of the just. And in this game, one speaks only inasmuch as one listens, that is, one speaks as a listener, and not as an author. It is a game without an author. In the same way as the speculative game of the West is a game without a listener, because the only listener tolerated by the speculative philosopher is the disciple. Well, what is a disciple? Someone who can become an author, who will be able to take the master's place. This is the only person to whom the master speaks. This is a pragmatic privilege; it sets the limits of a language game. So you see that all language games have rules, and these rules deal with the functioning of the various pragmatic positions. What you have just said about the prescriptive game shows that one of its basic rules is indeed that the position of sender must remain empty. No one may put herself or himself there; no one may be the authority.

JLT: Yes, but what is problematic for me is that we are speaking of a language game outside of an immanent functioning of this game.

JFL: Transcendence is immanent to the prescriptive game. This must be understood. What is being called the transcendence of the prescriptive is simply the fact that the position of the sender, as authority that obligates, is left vacant. That is, the prescriptive utterance comes from nothing: its pragmatic virtue of obligation results from neither its content nor its utterer.

JLT: And so it is because the recipient is taken ahold of, it is because one is taken ahold of by something that is beyond us that there is obligation. Or better: it is because it is beyond us and because it takes ahold of us that there is obligation.

Fifth Day
A Politics of Judgment

JFL: What we have said so far is a little uncertain, discontinuous, somewhat meticulous, but in the pejorative meaning of the term, a little obsessive also, and I have the same feeling you do. I think it comes from the fact that I am myself hesitant. To simplify: I hesitate between two positions, while still hoping that my hesitation is vain and that these are not two positions. To put it quickly, between a pagan position, in the sense of the Sophists, and a position that is, let us say, Kantian. I see quite well where their proximity lies: it is in the fact that there is no reason of history. I mean that no one can place himself or herself in the position of an utterer on the course of things. And therefore there is no court in which one can adjudicate the reason of history. This is a Kantian position if one thinks of the second Critique, or even of the third Critique. It is quite apparent what Kant is attempting to bring out in the second Critique: it is a language game that would be completely independent of that of knowledge. There is no knowledge in matters of ethics. And therefore there will be no knowledge in matters of politics. That is also the Sophists' position. And also Aristotle's, who, in matters of ethics and politics, follows the Sophists' problematic completely. In other words, there is no knowledge of practice. One cannot put oneself in a position of holding a discourse on the society; there are contingencies; the social web is made up of a multitude of encounters between interlocutors caught up in different pragmatics. One must judge case

73

by case. The position of the Sophists, at least some of them, called "conventionalism," asserts: It will be judged that it is just if it has been convened that that is what is just. I am not saying that all these positions are equivalent, far from it, but they all partake of a similar attitude toward what one could call "rationalist terrorism" in matters of history and political decisions. That is, it is not true that a political decision can be derived from a reason of history. I believe that this is the point that is at stake for us today, in the intelligentsia, at least the European one. That is what the debacle or the decadence of the Marxist narrative, as well as that of the liberal one, means specifically.

Put very briefly, this is how things hang together to the same side, I think. But within this regathering to one side, there are obviously considerable differences. And I would situate the divergence, if you will, by saying that it is the difference between a "philosophy" (but it is not a philosophy) of opinion and of the verisimilar that one finds among the Sophists, the Cynics, probably among the Skeptics, as well as in Aristotle, on one side; and on the other, a philosophy of Idea. This is where there is an essential political problem. To get back to our question of justice and of the prescriptive in ethical and in political matters, to follow the "philosophies" of opinion in their most banal, and probably most falsified, aspect, that is the so-called conventionalist philosophies of some Sophists, one would reach the very simple position that what is just in a collectivity of human beings at a given moment, is that which has been convened as just. But, locked in this frame, one loses all capacity to make the slightest judgment about what ought to be done. I believe that this was the sense of many of your questions. A rule by convention would require that one accept, let's get to the bottom of things right away, even Nazism. After all, since there was near unanimity upon it, from where could one judge that it was not just? This is obviously very troublesome. That is why it has been possible to call the Sophists opportunists, and to say that they were doing the ruling group's work. Personally, I don't think so, first, because there is a current of sophistic thought that does not go in this direction at all, and secondly, because it strikes as too hasty a reading, even of conventionalism. But let us accept it.

Now, if we look at it from the point of view of an Idea, in Kant's sense, in matters of ethics and politics, one can see quite readily that there is, on the contrary, a regulating Idea, that allows us, if not to decide in every specific instance, at least to eliminate in all cases (and independently of the convention of positive law), decisions, or, to put it in Kant's language, maxims of the will, that cannot be moral.

Once again, this regulating Idea is the Idea of a suprasensible nature, that is, of a totality of practical, reasonable beings. This is where my uncertainty lies. Wait, another important item needs to be specified: when Kant introduces the notion of Idea, and if one follows the course that this notion takes in his writings, from the dialectics of pure speculative reason through practical reason, and especially in the *Critique of Judgment*, and even more in light of our concerns here, in the texts on history, where it is fully utilized, if I may say so, well, this notion of Idea must never be confused with the notion of concept. It is always a reflective use of judgment, that is, a maximization of concepts outside of any knowledge of reality. So, the alternative is not a choice between a rational politics and a politics of opinion. That is not what is at stake. For me, rational politics, in the sense of the concept, is over, and I think that that is the swerve of this *fin-de-siècle*. We have had an attempt, since the Jacobins, to elaborate and implement a rational politics; this attempt has been pursued throughout the nineteenth century and most of the twentieth; it is presently collapsing. And that is a very good thing. When I say "pagan politics," I am obviously turning very explicitly toward the "lesser Greeks," that is, the Sophists: they have always indicated that we are dealing with what they called *phantasmata*, that is, representations, and that it is not true that a rational *knowledge* of social and political facts is possible, at least insofar as they imply judgments and decisions.

JLT: Is it then that you are doing a Kantian reading of these "lesser Greeks?"

JFL: The problem is indeed how to articulate this philosophy of opinions with the Kantian notion of Idea. For Kant, the Idea is not an opinion. The Idea is an almost unlimited use of the concept: one has concepts, and then one maximizes them. This is a notion that perhaps does not exist in ancient Greece. It presupposes a kind of time for research, I would say. A sort of field where one can run and let oneself go to see how far one can reach with a given concept. The notion of opinion is much more crude, at first sight, since it simply means, on one hand, that this is a thing that has "always" been said, that there are people to defend such a judgment, or that, in any case, those are things that one has "always" heard told, a throwback to the tradition of narratives (accepted things, customs); and on the other hand, and that is the Sophists', and Aristotle's, notion of opinion, that one speaks only within the realm of the verisimilar and one can never speak in the realm of the true. That is, even if one carries out rigorously a syllogism of opinion, since the premises are opinions, the conclusion will remain an opinion, notwithstanding the logical rigor. There are very precise forms for the derivation of opinions, but they do not get us out of the *eikos*, that is, from the verisimilar.

For Kant, an Idea does not appear to have anything to do with the verisimilar. It may even be completely lacking in verisimilitude. It does not rest at all upon a store constituted either by the narratives acknowledged in a popular community or by the great names recognized among a given people as those of sages. On the contrary, it rests upon something like the future of further inquiry: there is a free field left open to the reflective judgment's capability to go beyond the boundaries of sensible experience. My question then is: Can we have a politics without the Idea of justice? and if so, can we do so on the basis of opinion? If we remain with opinion, what will be just ultimately is that upon which people agree that it is just. It is common opinion. This is an extraordinarily dangerous position. If, on the contrary, we take a Kantian position, we have a regulator, that is a safekeeper of the pragmatics of obligation.

But then my question changes to the following: What relation can there be between what I call paganism on the one hand, and the Kantian Idea of a totality of reasonable beings, on the other. (I know that the expression "totality of reasonable beings" is antiquated, but, such as it is, it nonetheless says very well what I mean.) I see what this Idea of reasonable beings is going to become in Kant's politics, when it gets transcribed in the writings on history and on politics. It contributes to the article on Enlightenment; it contributes to the *Idea of a History from a Cosmopolitical Point of View*; it even contributes, by its negative side, to some rather deplorable remarks in *Theory and Practice* on the right to rebel, where more or less the following is said: after all, when there exists an established authority, it is entirely out of the question that another authority can be found in the name of which the first could be positively challenged; therefore, there is no positive right to revolt. I see quite well that it does indeed imply that one is always under the authority of the Idea, only of the Idea, and not that of the concept. But under the authority of the Idea implies a finality. And so the question I have been asking myself becomes finally: Can one engage in a politics without finality?

JLT: Yes. But, in a way, we are getting back to a question I have already asked you. If one admits this finality, this suprasensible world, doesn't one run into the postulate of the "counterpart" of the real world?

JFL: Yes, but this postulate is only postulated . . .

JLT: . . . As a horizon.

JFL: Yes, as a horizon. That's it. That is an Idea. . . .

JLT: That is an Idea, this world as Idea.

JFL: Simply an Idea, without any reality.

JLT: Right. Of course.

JFL: It is not even able to give us contents for prescriptions, but just regulates our prescriptives, that is, guides us in knowing what is just and what is not just. But guides us without, in the end, really guiding us, that is, without telling us what is just. By telling us: If one does such and such a thing, in the final analysis that is not compatible, if one reflects upon it in a reflective judgment, with the existence of a human society. Then, my problem is: To what extent is this game of the Idea pagan? There is a Sophistic tradition that goes in this direction. One finds texts by Antiphonius, for example, that go clearly in this direction, where it is said: There is no difference between the Barbarians and us; slaves are human beings. In other words, one finds statements that attempt to universalize the horizon of the Intersubjective pragmatics. What is the exact status of such statements in Antiphonius? Are they opinions? If they are opinions, they are reversible; they admit of counterexamples, like all opinions. When Kant presents practical universality as an Idea, he does not present it as an opinion; he presents it as the extension of the concept. And that implies that this Idea, which is not a concept, is nonetheless a reasonable idea. But also that, though it may be reasonable, it is not rational (in the sense of Hegel's *Philosophy of Right*, for example).

That is where we are. There is a general failure, quite impressive actually, a collapse of supposedly rational politics, sociality, and economics, and the field is open to two types of reading, I think. One would be a pagan reading in the sense of conventionalism. The question then would be: What can justice be under the rule of convention? There is a reading that is, let us say, Kantian, in which one sees quite clearly what justice can be but which presents another difficulty: to the extent that it links the Idea to reason, it does not present it as a language game, even though it does not present it as a metaphysics either. Even if Kant came, especially in the last writings, to take his idea of finality so seriously that it appears to exist, nonetheless all of this is, and must remain, of the order of the *als ob*, the "as if." How to interpret this "as if?" Is the Kantian "as if" always to be interpreted, following Kant himself, in opposition to the concept in its knowledgeable usage, an Idea never being more than an "as if" concept since it lacks an intuitionable reality to subsume? Or must we take Kant's "as if" in the sense of the Sophists? That is, as if it were reasonable, which is something else altogether. It is obvious that for Kant it is not "as if it were reasonable," *it is* reasonable. And, conversely, it is "as if" it were a concept, but *it is not* a concept.

See, in a text in the *Rhetoric*, Aristotle gives the argument of a Sicilian rhetorician that he connects to Protagoras's technique. The rhetorician defends a client who is very strong physically and who is accused of having battered a weak person. The person presenting the case to the judge, that is, the victim or his lawyer, says: "But he is very strong; it is obviously he who has beaten me!" The defense attorney offers the following refutation: "Of course not! My client knew very well that he would be accused because of his great strength, and it is precisely for that reason that he did not do it." Aristotle protests against this trick, this *tekhnè*. He says: "This is a *tekhnè* that is pure *tekhnè*; it does not have any rational power." I am wondering if our whole business does not lie in this sort of turn, a turn upon nothing at all. Could we not say that the judge who rejects this turn, this trick, is a judge who refuses the Idea? He refuses that the idea may have arisen to Corax's client, that it is precisely because of the tradition, that is, of the common opinion that requires that the stronger beat the weaker, that he has abstained from beating someone weaker. The judge refuses that the client may have had such an idea, that is, this type of anticipation, and, I would say, of maximization. So that in this Aristotelian version of the just, one feels the weight of opinion as the past, as a near truth acquired in the reckoning of a very frequent repetition of the judgment. The move, or the case, has been repeated, and, insofar as it has been repeated, it is likely (verisimilar) that it will be repeated. In the idea that Corax attributes to his client, even if it is presented as a *tekhnè*, there is already all of Kant, at least all of the Kant of the Idea: I am likely to be found guilty if opinion remains what it is, but if I maximize and if I use my imagination, if I anticipate what the judge will decide on the basis of common opinion, then I may be able to reverse the likelihood, the verisimilitude. In other words, it is the reasonable idea that produces what Aristotle calls the inverisimilar, the unlikely. Of course in saying this, one sides with the rhetorician against Aristotle's judge; one sides for Corax's client's reason against the reason of Aristotle's judge. And conversely, one could say, if Aristotle is to be believed, that Kant, if he is the Corax of the case, is a Sophist.

JLT: Yes, but to maximize opinions is one thing; to maximize concepts, another. To maximize concepts, that is an Idea. . . .

JLF: Ah! But of course!

JLT: And to maximize opinions, what is that?

JFL: In Kantian terms, you are right; you are a thousand times right. Anyway, in Kantian terms, there are no opinions. One does not concern oneself with them, in any case.

JLT: Well how does one maximize opinion? How does one introduce opinion into the Kantian register?

JFL: Well, insofar as this opinion will find itself involved in a language game that is a conflict, properly speaking, a dialectical conflict, in Aristotle's sense, or a rhetorical conflict (it is the same as far as we are concerned here), when this opinion, then, will find itself mobilized as an argument, as a weapon, in a conflict with an adversary, to maximize it then, and actually it is much more than maximizing it (the term is not a happy one), it can be to transform it; in our case, it means that it undergoes a negative transformation in the logical sense. It is appealed to in the argument: it is precisely *because* you say that it is always the strong who beat the weak, that I did not beat this weaker individual.

JLT: Yes.

JFL: Here we have the anticipation of a decision that is not yet taken but that will likely be taken in order *not to have* it be taken. The difference between Aristotle's judge and Corax, is that Corax introduces, into the use of opinions, the future, and notably here the future of the decision of the judge who will rely upon past opinions. Corax anticipates a judge who, on the contrary, is always in a regressive position vis-à-vis the ongoing, who, in other words, relies upon the *already judged* in order to establish and judge the fact. Whereas Corax relies upon the *not yet judged* to establish precisely that an act did not take place.

JLT: Yes, he anticipates an opinion.

JFL: Precisely. But this opinion is nonetheless a synthetic judgment. It is empirical, but it is a synthetic judgment that asserts that ordinarily the stronger beat the weaker. The client is supposed to have anticipated this probability and to have therefore prevented himself from beating the weaker person because of what the judge was going to decide, in order not to fall under the judge's law. It is a ruse in relation to a law. This law, as is always the case both for Aristotle and the Sophists, is nothing but a custom. It can be turned. It suffices to anticipate it. Anticipation alone allows the reversal of the expected relation: thanks to it, the stronger has refrained from beating the weaker, and has thus made himself as weak or even weaker than he. We are of course in the midst of a ruse. But it seems to me that we are also in something else that does not work without the category of finality, to use Kantian terms. One could say indeed that the cause of the innocence of the client, provided Corax tells the truth, is precisely the effect that the reverse of this cause would have, that is, the condemnation he was risking if he had beaten the victim. The effect would have been the verdict of the judge, and it is this effect that holds the client back from perpetrating violence upon the weak one. So here Corax's argument does not work unless one brings in an anticipation, and through it, an ideality (the unreality: the effect that would have ensued) and a finality.

JLT: A finality?

JFL: Corax conducts his argument in relation to a sort of idea of the use to which opinions will be put, especially by the judge. He tells himself: "But careful now. In matters of opinion, precisely because one is in opinion, the reverse of what is believed and holds sway as law is nonetheless not refutable and can therefore be defended." It is quite easy to see how Corax plays on the dialectical fact that from an opinion one can produce the opposite opinion, and that one can use this faculty in a situation that is agonistic. To be sure, it is not the same as in the case of the concept, but if one starts to maximize concepts, one will rapidly find oneself in what Kant himself calls sophisms, notably the antinomies and the paralogisms of reason in its dialectical usage.

One can demonstrate both the thesis and the antithesis of an antinomy. Well, isn't that the case with opinions? After all, the Sophist in the *Dissoi Logoi* [*Two Discourses*] does nothing else but demonstrate "black" on one page and "white" on the next. And so you see, I wonder whether we should not reread; I try to go forward in this dangerous undertaking that is the Dialectic in the first *Critique*, which is so important since the other two *Critiques* stem from it. I try to reread it in a dialectical perspective, in Aristotle's sense, that is in fact, in the sophistic sense, because that is where the political field opens up.

But it opens up in two ways, and that is where I get back to the subject of my hesitation. On the one hand, it opens up as a *field of ruses*, that is, of reverse argumentations, of which Corax's turn is but an example among many others. But, on the other hand, in Kant, the political field necessarily opens up as the *field of finality* in the broadest sense. There prevails there the Idea of something that is not yet here, that will never be here (for Kant, it is clear that the intuition that would correspond to it will never obtain in experience) but that suffices to regulate what is to be done. So, two elements: a field of ruses, a field of finality. I can see how one can map out the field of ruses in Kant, how one can introduce eristics in it, or agonistics in any case, and that is the space of the dialectic in the second half of the *Critique of Pure Reason*. My problem is to figure out where is finality among the Sophists and the rhetoricians. It seems to me that this type of operation, which I am presenting in an ostensibly scholarly fashion, but which actually has a very immediate political upshot, can be performed, and it will then be possible to give the word "pagan" its full meaning. Because then it would include justice, and a justice that would not be merely unanimous convention, which is something that cannot be tolerated.

JLT: It seems to me that you are facing the following problem: you would like to maximize opinions, whereas there is no finality in the field of opinions.

JFL: Exactly. One could put it that way. If one limits oneself to the notion of opinion or that of representation, of *phantasma* in other words, then it seems to me that the combination is impossible. In such a hypothesis, there is no morality, or, if one introduces morality, it risks being but a morality by convention, where, as Pascal rightly says, what is just is that which has been judged as just and upon which everyone agrees. And it is true that, under those conditions, there is no possible politics. There is only consensus. But we know what that means: the manufacture of a subject that is authorized to say "we."

JLT: I would like to come back to what you have just said and to indicate more clearly how I view things. It is quite clear that today a rational politics is no longer admissible. I mean by that the project of a science of politics must be abandoned. Politics is not a matter of science. Then, the only tenable position, as far as I am concerned, is one that I would call a "politics of judgment," a sort of "critique of political judgment." In other words, a politics that would admit that its realm is that of opinions. The problem one runs into then is the following: How do I decide among opinions if I no longer accept as legitimate the appeal to science? The question must be asked: Where do I get this capability to judge? If all opinions are acceptable, then I cannot decide. For instance, in the name of what do I lean toward Aristotle rather than toward Plato? This is where the *Critique of Judgment* becomes of interest to me. I propose that we overlook that it is a critique of the feeling of pleasure and pain, and consider it exclusively as a critique of feeling, and I further propose to translate feeling by the simple assertion: *I am for, I am against, yes, no*. Assent granted or denied. I think that it is this sort of feeling that is put into play by any political judgment.

JFL: There is no politics of reason, neither in the sense of a totalizing reason nor in that of the concept. And so we must do with a politics of opinion. And what you are proposing, and it does seem to me to be very important in relation to the discussion of the other day, is to take out this opinion from the overly empirical context that many Sophists (and even Aristotle) have given to it, and to grant it the scope of what is called judgment in Kant, that is, the capability of thinking outside of the concept and outside of habit.

JLT: Absolutely.

JFL: I'll "buy" it, if I may put it this way. . . . This proposition must be weighed; it must be evaluated. Does it hold up? Or is it a theoretical and practical monster? It is somewhat what I was trying to suggest by means of my Corax example, namely, that what passes for a paradox—I get back to this matter of the paradox, because it is a big thing; the paradox is the hot spot of this business—what passes for a paradox, or a sophistry, then, or a paralogism in matters of opinion, is often, and perhaps generally, an Ideal usage, in the Kantian sense, of opinion. Which means, the capability to decide (the recourse to the capability of decision) in the diversity of opinions and not merely by means of what has been attained. This is where the whole matter lies: one must not merely take into consideration all of society as a sensible nature, as an ensemble that already has its laws, its customs, and its regularities; but the capability to decide by means of what is adjudged as to be done, by taking society as a suprasensible nature, as something that is not there, that is not given. Then the direction of opinion will be reversed: it is not taken any more as a sediment of facts of judgment and behavior; it is weighed from a capability that exceeds it and that can be in a wholly paradoxical position with respect to the data of custom. In such a case, it is quite clear that there are two ways of deciding outside of rational criteria. I think that is what you were suggesting with Aristotle's judge. It happens that he hesitates to decide when he is dealing with opinions that are exactly contrary to each other, especially if, as happens with Kant's antinomic theses, both are perfectly demonstrable. Or he decides according to the specific weight of each opinion and finds in favor of the "heavier" one, the one more commonly shared; or he decides by guiding himself by means of a sort of horizon, a horizon of justice. But then the question is: What is it that such a horizon allows us to discern? Can one say what is the idea of the totality of reasonable beings? Can it be given a "content," even if it be a purely formal one, that woud let us say: This conduct, or that utterance, is not just, whereas this one is? Whatever the answer, it is paradoxical in relation to the system of opinions, because it always implies that there is a sort of reversal in the "use" of time. What allows us to decide is not that which has been attained, but that which remains to be attained; it is ahead of us, like an Idea. But we must not lose sight of the essential: even if we admit that the paradoxes of the Sophists, or of the rhetoricians, or those of the Megaratics, imply a use of the Idea, that is, of time, and the localization of a horizon of things to be done in order to judge things already done, the problem of knowing how this horizon is to be defined remains whole, since there is no possible knowledge of it.

Sixth Day
The Faculty of Political Ideas

JLT: Why can't we have a politics of practical reason? Why must we appeal, as it seems to me that we must, to judgment to regulate politics? Why, if not because the concept of freedom is determinant here. It legislates.

JFL: To say that it is determinant . . . Kant said it was not determinant. To begin with, freedom is a concept that is not conceivable, that is what Kant says. It is rather a force, an entity that is presupposed as a source of law but one does not have any experience of it.

JLT: It does determine the will, however.

JFL: No, it does not determine even the will. It does not determine the will inasmuch as it is the will in its pure state. It is transcendental freedom. But it does not determine it in the sense of determination in speculative reason; in other words, it does not determine it the way a cause determines an effect. It determines it only the way a teleological idea *regulates* a conduct, which is something altogether different. It is for this reason that the moral law has no content. If freedom determined the maxim of the will, the latter would have a content. In practical matters, there would be sensible intuitions to put under the laws enunciated by freedom, that is, under the obligations. But there is no content to the law. And if there is no content, it is precisely because freedom is not determinant. Freedom is regulatory; it appears in the statement of the law only as that which must be respected; but one must always reflect in order to know if in repaying a loan or in refusing to give away a friend, etc., one is actually acting, *in every single instance*, in such a way as to maintain the Idea of a society of free beings.

JLT: Yet, freedom must give its law to nature.

JFL: But it is incapable of placing intuitions under its concept.

JLT: Yes, of course. But to have a politics of practical reason takes us back to the hypothesis of a suprasensible world and this suprasensible world is supposed to legislate; it must exercise its power over nature.

JFL: Well, that seems to me both true and false. Like you, and by the way it is something that I have tried to show in a text on Lévinas, I think that there is a sort of return of the denotative in the very heart of Kant's prescriptive statements. After all, the expression "so that" does imply a statement that you would call "metaphysical," defining what suprasensible nature is, namely, the totality of practical, reasonable beings. And it is true that everything leads one to such a conclusion. Nonetheless, upon a second look, I would say — and here I would be rather critical with respect to what I wrote in that text — there is however the famous *so dass* [so that] of the imperative that does not say: "If you want to be this, then do that," which is a determining effect and which Kant eliminates on the ground of its being a hypothetical imperative. The *so dass* marks the properly reflective use of judgment. It says: Do whatever, not on condition that, but *in such a way as* that which you do, the maxim of what you do, can always be valid as, etc. We are not dealing here with a determinant synthesis but with an Idea of human society. And that is very different. It is an Idea. It is not a concept that determines; it is a concept in its reflective, and only in its reflective, use. Which means, and you know this as well as I do, that this use ultimately *leaves* the conduct to be adopted *un*determined. Suprasensible nature *does not* determine *what* I have to do. It regulates me, but without telling me *what* there is to be done. This is what Kant calls formalism (a very poor term, as far as I am concerned).

JLT: There is a misunderstanding. What I mean to say is that reason has the power to legislate, that is, simply that it is practical by itself.

JFL: We get back here to the distinction for which Kant has been irreplaceable, to me at least, that is, the distinction between prescriptives and denotatives. In its speculative use, reason determines because it proceeds by means of denotations, that is, by syntheses determinant of referents. In its practical use, reason determines only a pragmatics; it does not determine a content. Reason issues a command that is not even valid by its content, but insofar as it elicits obligation. No law of nature obliges us. Only the law of reason in its practical use obligates. But this obligation is not a determination in Kant's sense of the term. And that means that Kant distinguishes perfectly well between statements that are denotative and that give (or do not give; but in the Transcendental Analytics, they do give) knowledge, and utterances that are prescriptive and determine nothing, because they have no relation to knowledge. It is not accurate then to say that reason is, in such a case, determinant in practical use. It situates a pragmatics, and the latter is different from the pragmatics of denotations.

JLT: The starting point for my comments is the fact that the *Critique of Practical Reason* is not concerned with moral judgment, with the "case by case"; it refers to the capacity that reason has, all by itself and without the aid of any other faculty, to provide a rule for my actions.

JFL: One must judge that the maxim of what one is doing is compatible with suprasensible nature. But we don't actually know this because it is not subject to knowledge, for the excellent reason that we are dealing here with suprasensible nature and the latter does not admit of knowledge. It is very simple. One does not know what this nature is. Where I get the sense of your question is somewhere else, not at this level, not with respect to determination. It is at the level of something like a horizon, something that is indexed by the return of the idea of totality. When Kant introduces as a regulator for the determination of actions by means of reflection, the Idea of a suprasensible nature, that is, of a society of free and responsible beings, he is indeed introducing the Idea of a totality. This is where I see one of your presuppositions, namely, that the world forms a totality. That is true. And then he projects it (or rejects it) under the form of an Idea, an Idea that will never have a corresponding intuition, so that humanity will always be asymptotic to this Idea. But nonetheless it goes without saying for Kant—and it is very clear in the article on Enlightenment, and in *The Cosmopolitical Idea*, or in the *Project of Perpetual Peace*—that humanity must form a whole. Isn't that so?

JLT: Once again I have the feeling that you are equating the *Critique of Judgment* with the *Critique of Practical Reason*. Whereas I was trying to distinguish between the two. In one we are dealing with a philosophy of will, whereas in the other we have a philosophy of judgment. My concern with their distinction comes from the hypothesis that in matters of justice, if it is true that we are in the realm of opinions, we have to have recourse to another faculty than the will. We must discriminate and not determine a field. And I see only judgment to allow us to do that.

JFL: Kant indeed uses the term "causality" to speak of the relation of the will to its effects. But he acknowledges that this causality has nothing to do with the "horizontal" causality, if I may call it that, that can be synthesized in the statements of speculative reason, that is, in those of knowledge. The causality in question is the source of incredible misunderstandings; it really is a leftover from the Humean tradition. This causality of the will is not an empirical causality.

JLT: Of course not. But what will be the end of Practical Reason? To produce a world that will be in conformity with thought. For that reason, it is a philosophy of the will.

JFL: But it will never be known whether it is in conformity.

JLT: Perhaps it can never be achieved. . . .

JFL: Precisely because we are dealing with an Idea of nature and not with chains of causality under which intuitions can be subsumed. Therefore, it is not true to say that this totality, that the thought of this totality, determines a given action, in the sense that the sun shining on a stone determines its being warm.

JLT: No, of course not.

JFL: But that is a determination in the strict sense of the term. The principle of universal legislation, which is nothing but the totality of suprasensible beings, cannot function as determinant in the statement of the moral law. It can only function as Idea. However, the judgment is not absolutely undetermined, and here I again link up with what you were saying: it is presupposed that this Idea is the idea of a totality. Whereas the problem that faces us, even if it is put in terms of Idea and reflective judgment, is that it is no longer a matter, for us, of reflecting upon what is just or unjust against the horizon of a social totality, but, on the contrary, against the horizon of a multiplicity or of a diversity.

JLT: Very good.

JFL: This is where both practical reason and political reason are still beholden, in Kant, to metaphysics, because of this idea of totality. But it is not a metaphysics, at least in the Kantian sense, because it is an Idea and not a concept. This is where I would operate a divide, at my own risk, because I am not certain that I am in the strict Kantian tradition.

In other words, to resume our discussion where we left it, I believe that it is now a matter of doing a politics of opinions that would give us the capacity of deciding between opinions and of distinguishing between what is just and what is not just; and to have this capacity of deciding, one must effectively have an Idea; but, in contradistinction to what Kant thought, this Idea is not, for us today, an Idea of totality.

JLT: Allow me to return to this. Does recourse to Practical Reason suffice to decide between opinions?

JFL: If I get back to the distinction you were proposing a while ago, it is true that one can seek the support of the *Critique of Practical Reason*, and in that sense you are right. One cannot do so insofar as it is a transcendental analysis of the conditions of possibility of obligation in general and of those of morality. It provides no support because, and only because, the analysis is a transcendental one. There is lacking an empirical ethics (an ethics of "prudence"), that is, a politics. There is lacking not quite a fourth "Critique" but a third part to the third *Critique*. One can wonder at the fact that, in the third *Critique*, reflective judgment is at work only on the aesthetic object and nature as teleology. Because there is yet another realm to which reflective judgment obviously applies: the realm of political society. If Kant had followed up the Critique of Practical Reason with a "Critique of Political Reason," he would have been forced to adopt the viewpoint of an Aristotelian judge. In any case, whenever Kant had further occasion to discuss the *Critique of Practical Reason*, it has been casuistry. Such is the case with the right to lie, for example. It so happens that Aristotle's judge, the political in general, are in casuistry, therefore in opinion. But then, the question is: Do we still have, in opinion itself, that is, in the particular case, the faculty of judging? We do have the faculty of judging. And it is not pleasure and pain because we are in the political.

JLT: It is not pleasure and pain that make me judge.

JFL: Okay. Good. Then what is it?

JLT: It is the Idea.

JFL: It is the Idea.

JLT: It is precisely in the realm of concrete ethics, of the particular instance, that the problem of judgment cannot fail to arise with considerable acuity as well as necessity. When it is a question of acceptance or of refusal, and that is what the domain of feeling is for me (the domain of yes/no). But I don't have to say yes or no to the transcendental. This is what I mean earlier by one must not do a philosophy of the will.

JFL: What are you thinking of when you say that one must not do a philosophy of the will? Do you mean it in the Kantian or in the Nietzschean sense?

JLT: A philosophy of the will yields a world that imposes its law upon another, or else it can go as far as saying—and then the unification can be total—that it is the will that produces both worlds, as happens in Nietzsche.

JFL: Yes, I agree.

JLT: Instead, on the contrary, of having the will keep open the "abyss" between the two worlds.

JFL: I said I agreed, but with considerable regret. After all, what I tried to do for some time was just that.

JLT: That brings us back to a previous conversation.

JFL: Yes, and it is not worth returning to. . . .

JLT: I was telling you then that you were abandoning the point of view of a philosophy of the will.

JFL: Yes. And what did I answer?

JLT: "Yes," it seems to me.

JFL: Yes, because—you understand, and it really is not worth getting back to it—but the point of view of the will, what does it mean in politics? That is the heart of the matter. If you will, I am almost tempted to say now that this philosophy of the will, as it is expressed in a manner that is at once, how shall I put it, baroque, sophisticated, and expressionistic in *L'Economie libidinale*, has been a sort of purgatory. It was a matter of ridding political reflection of Hegelianism, of purging it of this modern version of Hegelianism that is constituted, for me, by Lacanism, to purge it from the finally determinant use of concepts that is called "semiotics," and of a Marxism of the Althusserian type, let us say; well, not only, of Marx's Marxism as well, so as to relieve a philosophy of the tremendous weight of the various politics of reason and of the philosophies of reason. And so in the book, a truly opposite position has been taken in resolute fashion, something that has been deplored by quite a few. . . . It remains that I had to go through it, that is all. Now, I am trying to get back to this issue. I have never abandoned it; I try to get back to it indirectly. But it is true that a philosophy of the will cannot be passed, as such, for a political philosophy. It does not work.

JLT: Right.

JFL: The other day I was rereading some passages in Dufrenne. It is not true that one can do an aesthetic politics. It is not true the search for intensities or things of that type can ground politics, because there is the problem of injustice. It is not true, for example, that once one has gotten rid of the primacy of the understanding in its knowing function, there is only aesthetic judgment left to discriminate between the just and the unjust. Aesthetic judgment allows the discrimination of that which pleases from that which does not please. With justice, we have to do, of necessity, with the regulation of something else.

JLT: That was not the point of view of intensities. It was not the point of view of that which pleases or does not please.

JFL: Quite so, but that is Dufrenne's interpretation.

JLT: Any philosophy of the will—and it is quite summary to put it this way—inevitably gets into matters of velocity (slowdowns, acceleration, sedimentation), since, ultimately, it is a monistic philosophy.

JFL: That's right.

JLT: And since it is monistic, differences can be found only by means of ratios of velocities, with the idea that, by putting the syntheses into play, one will modify or one will transform the whole.

JFL: Yes, and actually that was the role that the idea of the death instinct, as I took it from *Beyond the Pleasure Principle*, played for me.

JLT: Yes, that's right. As an untying, as a loosening up.

JFL: Quite. And as acceleration. They are the same as the life instincts, but in a hurry. It is a difference of rhythm.

JLT: It is a politics that I would call "American," if you will.

JFL (laughter): Yes, it is quite broadly a politics of capital, actually. That is true. And I think that what interested me, was to see it at work within capital, to make it appear in its affirmative force. Except that, insofar as one is a political thinker, one cannot do without justice. But the question is: What is this horizon? Which horizon are we determining?

JLT: Do you think that we could risk the formula that justice is the faculty of political ideas?

JFL: It is not the faculty of political ideas. I think that it is a regulatory idea in the political arena, but I don't think that it can be said that it is the faculty itself. The faculty itself, does it have a name? If it does, the name should evoke more the pragmatics of the social bond, I should think. It would be rather the faculty of the social bond. And the question is whether this faculty is regulated by an idea or not, and this idea, which can only be that of justice, what is its content? Otherwise, it is as if you were saying that freedom is the faculty of willing. It is not true. But it is the idea that the faculty of willing needs to regulate itself.

JLT: Yes, but I meant the formula on the model of this one: "Genius, the faculty of aesthetic ideas."

JFL: Oh, yes, in that sense. . . .

JLT: The just one would be the one who would have the faculty of producing political ideas.

JFL: In that sense, yes.

JLT: Actually, this individual would be regulated by the Idea. . . .

JFL: Yes, in that sense. Basically this is what the Hassidim could say, with their perfect concern (and considerable intelligence in the matter) for making very clear that the content of this idea is not given, that this law is not determinant, and that one never knows. There is no knowledge of what the law says. Which is the general fate of the political. But at the same time that it does not give any knowledge (this idea of justice neither determines nor is determined by any knowledge), nonetheless, we, we have to try to define its content. When Kant says "totality of reasonable beings" (I know that he is talking about morality, but he transcribes this in the opuscula, which are, to some extent, the unwritten third part of the *Critique of Judgment*), he rewrites this totality under the form of a pacified humanity, something like the League of Nations. Well, I am presently reading the texts that Buber gathered under the name *Gog and Magog*, and that are Hassidic narratives contemporaneous with the French Revolution and with Bonapartism. And it is very interesting to see how Buber has the first great Tsadikim, the Hassidic sages, talk about the Jacobinic idea. That is, in a certain way, to talk in relation to something that is, in political history, akin to some of Kant's ideas at least (some, by no means all; for example, there is the idea of democracy, which is profoundly distasteful to Kant). There is here a very interesting short circuit because the Just of the Hassidic tradition rise up against Jacobinism, saying that it is madness to know the just.

JLT: It is the determinant use of the Idea.

JFL: There you are. It is Terror all over again. Terror in the name of freedom. Because as soon as one makes a determinant use of the Idea, then it is necessarily the Terror. And then the content of the Idea matters little. This use of the Idea of freedom and of obligation has led to the attribution to Kant of what, in all justice, should be attributed to Robespierre and to the Jacobins. Perhaps your, our, reservations with respect to Practical Reason are unconsciously governed by the presumption that it leads to Terror. . . .

Seventh Day
Majority Does Not Mean
Great Number But Great Fear

JFL: I would like to come back to a specific point. In Kant, the idea that will be used as the regulator of the decision of justice is that of a unity or of a totality. In morality, the totality of reasonable beings; in politics, the unity of humanity, at least humanity from a cosmopolitical point of view or, again, pacified humanity. I think this idea of Idea has to be gotten back to. Impossible to enter into the political area without having the question of justice raised. Here I see several things that differentiate us completely from the way in which problem is set in Kant. First I see that, to pick up our terminology, if one has the viewpoint of a multiplicity of language games, if one has the hypothesis that the social bond is not made up of a single type of statement, or, if you will, of discourse, but that it is made up of several kinds of these games, of which a certain number is known, then it follows that, to put it quickly, social partners are caught up in pragmatics that are different from each other. And this multiple belonging, this belonging to several pragmatics, can manifest itself rather quickly; it is not a problem of empirical diachrony; in the same discussion one goes, one leaps, from one language game to another, from the interrogative to the prescriptive, and so on. Each of these language games operates a distribution of roles, if one can put it this way. Actually, it is even more complicated than that, because there are variants within the language games. Let us simplify; let us say that there is a distribution of roles that is effected by the narrative game; there is a distribution of roles (which has nothing to do with the one of the narrative) that is effected by the prescriptive (even if there are prescriptions implied in the narration). Actually there is, I would not even say a weaving, because a weaving requires a unity of thread, but a patchwork of language pragmatics that vibrate at all times. And that means that the partners, the people who are assigned their roles by the language games in which they are caught, occupy positions that are incommensurable to each other. Not only is there an incommensurability within a game between the position of recipient and that of utterer, for example (it is not always pronounced, but it is extreme in the case of obligation), but, from game to game, for the "same" position, there is incommensurability: it is not the same thing to be the recipient of a narrative, and to be the recipient of a denotative discourse with a function of truthfulness, or to be the recipient of a command.

The picture that one can draw from this observation is precisely that of an absence of unity, an absence of totality. All of this does not make up a body. On the contrary. And the idea that I think we need today in order to make decisions in political matters cannot be the idea of the totality, or of the unity, of a body. It can only be the idea of a multiplicity or of a diversity. Then the question arises: How can a regulatory use of this idea of the political take place? How can it be pragmatically efficacious (to the point where, for example, it would make one decision just and another unjust)? Is a politics regulated by such an idea of multiplicity possible? Is it possible to decide in a just way in, and according to, this multiplicity? And here I must say that I don't know.

For Kant, the idea of justice is associated with that of finality. But "finality" means a kind of convergence, of organization, of a general congruence, on the part of a given multiplicity moving toward its unity; even if it is in asymptotic and infinite fashion, without ever being able to tell: Here we are, the body is constituted and the unity accomplished. Nonetheless, there is this congruence, and it is presupposed in the statement of the moral law as the principle of universal legislation. The universality that appears here is actually the return of the idea of totality within the moral law. If we abandon this idea of congruence and we put in its stead the idea of a "discrepancy," the question then is whether one can have a moral law and a political law with it. "Always act in such a way that the maxim of your will may" I won't say "not be erected," but it is almost that, "into a principle of universal legislation." Into a principle of a multiplicity. . . .

JLT: Yes, but if you adopt this formulation, then you fall back into . . .

JFL: . . . of course . . .

JLT: . . . necessarily, into the horizon of unity and of totality.

JFL: Yes, that's right, but why? Does it come from the use of the "in such a way as to" that carries finality within itself, a unitary finality? That is a question. This is perhaps where one would have to reintroduce the notion of opinion that comes to us from the Sophists, but not with its load of past, custom, and received authority that has been focused on until now, but with its other load, multiplicity. It is equally present in someone like Protagoras, or even someone like Aristotle when he is busy describing some hundred constitutions from around the Mediterranean. To undertake a census of all these constitutions does imply an acceptance of the diversity among the forms of organization and a rejection of the notion of a congruence among them. Whatever he may have been in relation to the Macedonian empire, Aristotle did not posit a unity as the general horizon of these constitutions. He is satisfied to do here what, at first sight, appears to be an entomologist's job, but is actually more complicated. Aristotle knows very well that there is neither judge nor political justice without there being someone or something that decides, or has the capability of deciding, the capability of judging, and that one does not decide well without *phronèsis* [understanding]. And he knows that the *phronèsis* is spoken differently in each of these constitutions. Can there be then a plurality of justices? Or is the idea of justice the idea of a plurality? That is not the same question. I truly believe that the question we face now is that of a plurality, the idea of a justice that would at the same time be that of a plurality, and it would be a plurality of language games.

But what can this mean in practice? To state that one must draw a critique of political judgment means today to do a politics of opinions that, at the same time, is a politics of Ideas, as you attempted to synthesize it, something that, already, is not easy, but in addition it must be a politics of Ideas in which justice is not placed under a rule of convergence but rather a rule of divergence. I believe that this is the theme that one finds constantly in present-day writing under the name of "minority." Basically, minorities are not social ensembles; they are territories of language. Every one of us belongs to several minorities, and what is very important, none of them prevails. It is only then that we can say that the society is just. Can there be justice without the domination of one game upon the others?

JLT: I think that a politics that would regulate itself by the idea of minority and plurality, and that would propose to develop minorities in such a way that no minority could ever become a majority, and, on the contrary, that all majorities become minorities, and such a politics would renew the very difficulties you were recalling yourself but a while ago. It seems to run into the difficulties of monistic philosophy, of a philosophy of the will. Since any and every minority can be just. The only justice will be that no minority is to prevail upon any other.

JFL: Yes. You are flagging a difficulty, and one does risk falling back into a sort of indifferentism that is the bad side of the pagan line I am trying to trace. I think that the difficulty comes from this: when one thinks of justice according to a nonunitary teleology, one tends to merely reverse what was implied in Kant's doctrine, whereas one should be on one's guard, I think, against the totalitarian character of an idea of justice, even a pluralistic one.

The question you are asking is: What type of relation is there between justice and the various language games? One cannot simply be indifferent to the content of the language game. Here we can specify this: in the end, a game like the narrative game or like the descriptive-denotative game, is a game that is played by its own rules, and I maintain that it is not possible to judge from the point of view of justice (from the point of view of justice, right? that is, from a point of view that is specific to the prescriptive game), it is not possible to decide from the viewpoint of the prescriptive game about matters of denotative or narrative games. So, from this point of view, if one remains within these games (the narrative, the denotative, or any other) that are not prescriptive, the idea of justice does not have to intrude.

It intervenes inasmuch as these games are impure. By which I mean something very specific: inasmuch as these games are infiltrated by prescriptions. If a narrative has the value of a prescriptive, that is, if it claims to prescribe or if it appears to legitimate prescriptions, or if a denotative discourse presenting itself as scientific contains or implies prescriptions as well, something that happens frequently in the case of "experts" in modern capitalist society, then, in such cases, one can say that the game is impure, and it is clear that, at that moment, its effects must be regulated by the Idea of justice. Here the Idea of justice will consist in preserving the purity of each game, that is, for example, in insuring that the discourse of truth be considered as a "specific" language game, that narration be played by its "specific" rules. To the extent that these language games are accompanied by prescriptions of the type "repeat me" or "carry me out" or "implement me," then the idea of justice must regulate these obligations.

It is by means of plurality that it regulates them; it says, "Careful! There is *pléonexia* here, there is excess, there is abuse." The person holding this discourse of knowledge, playing this knowledge game, or the person playing this narrative game, is exceeding the authority granted to her or to him by the rules of the game and is not abiding by the pragmatics "proper" to the game played, for example, the pragmatics that rules the game of the one who knows with the one who listens and will get to know—the master-and-disciple-game —or the pragmatics rules the game of the one who tells with the one who listens. And she or he is introducing another pragmatics, that of prescriptions. You see, this pragmatics belongs actually to justice, to the Idea of justice. But the Idea of justice resides precisely in keeping prescription in its "proper" order, just as it does in keeping narration and description in the order that is respectively "proper" to them. That is, it consists in maintaining them as different games that cannot have the value of sources of universal obligation. Just as being just is independent of telling the truth, so telling a story, in and of itself, has nothing to do with justice. I think that this is the direction that I would go in.

JLT: I think that this is a first point, but there remains another question: Once the games have been restored to their purity, one still must discriminate between just and unjust prescriptives. I would like you, therefore, to get back to the Idea that regulates justice, the Idea of multiplicity. And I would like to see how it would work among the Hassidim, because it seems to me, that, among them, one does not find the idea of a justice regulated by the image of a homogeneous and complete social body. I think that this detour could allow us to specify the type of the multiple, the type of Idea that regulates justice in this case. You cited earlier the judgment of the Jewish Just upon the Jacobins, the empire, and upon the French Revolution. I think we would have there a very good example of a just evaluation.

JFL: Yes, at least if Buber is to be believed in the narratives of *Gog and Magog*; the Hassidic masters judge Jacobinism very severely. And the severity of the judgment is aimed at this sort of infatuation with wanting to issue prescriptions for the totality of the social body, that is, with wanting to achieve the unity of the community, with effecting the community. And there are some dialogues that are full of humor with respect to the possibility of ever achieving a community, including a Hassidic one. In a way, the community will never be achieved. What they discern is not only that the Jacobinic game is unjust in the immediate sense, but that it is unjust in a second sense: Robespierre intends to prescribe upon everything, that is, he intends to extend the sway of the Idea of justice to the totality of discourses and conducts. He does not respect the plurality of language games. At least that is how I understand his condemnation by the Hassidim.

If you will, one could look at the problem in another way, through humor. The relation to plurality is tied up with humor, in the case of Hassidism. For example, one tells a little story; the question is going to be whether there is, hidden in this little story, a prescription of any importance. The humor that is going to come in will show that the distance from the story one started out with to a given prescription is always immense. That is, the prescription is always transcendental, what I was calling "proper" a while ago. It can never be derived. And therefore the question of prescription will always remain an open question. There are no criteria, in the sense of a group of functors, and that is the specificity of this language game that implies prescription and obligation. There are no criteria because the idea of criteria comes from the discourse of truth and supposes a referent or a "reality" and, by dint of this, it does not belong to the discourse of justice. This is very important. It must be understood that if one wants criteria in the discourse of justice one is tolerating de facto the encroachment of the discourse of justice by the discourse of truth.

JLT: I wonder whether the position of the Hassidim does not come from their rather subtle conception of language. It seems to me that the idea is as follows: language cannot be mastered. It is something that I do not manipulate; in a way it comes to me from elsewhere; it does not come from me. In the end, I have the impression that their question is always: What does language want of me? Perhaps we could then specify further this idea of a multiple justice or at least of a justice that does not constitute a body.

JFL: You are absolutely right. It is indeed: What does language want of me? And in my idiom, it means that there are forms of language that are not forms of statements, that are forms of language games, that is, ways of playing that language has, that position the person who enters into the game. This person may enter here or there, he or she will be positioned by the game; in this sense, language is indeed not, and cannot be, mastered. Its very plurality makes it impossible for anyone to establish her- or himself in a field and proceed to produce its laws in a sort of universal language or generalized metalanguage, and then go on to extend these laws to all the fields of language. In this tradition, there is very clearly an awareness that there are several classes or ways of talking, and that, in any case, the efficacy of these ways of talking varies from language game to language game (from narration to prescription, for example, between which the distance is infinite). There is further the awareness that one cannot signify that which tells itself as a prescription other than in narrations, which does not prevent the fact that at the same time one will never be able to extract this prescription out of narrations in the form of semantic content. That is why it is just to maintain this plurality. And any attempt to state the law, for example, to place oneself in the position of enunciator of the universal prescription is obviously infatuation itself and absolute injustice, in point of fact.

And so, when the question of what justice consists in is raised, the answer is: "It remains to be seen in each case," and always in humor, but also in worry, because one is never certain that one has been just, or that one can ever be just. And that is due to this specific language game that includes prescription and obligation, whereas one can be certain of having been true. That, one can be relatively certain of; not absolutely but relatively: it is neither unthinkable nor absurd to think that one can have relative certainty in matters of truth. Can one be certain of being a good narrator? Perhaps. . . .

The capital issue is terror (not war, as Kant thinks). It is the fact that the social bond, understood as the multiplicity of games, very different among themselves, each with its own pragmatic efficacy and its capability of positioning people in precise places in order to have them play their parts, is traversed by terror, that is, by the fear of death. In a way, that has always been the political problem. The question of the social bond, when it is put in political terms, has always been raised in the form of a possible interruption of the social bond, which is simply called "death" in all of its forms: imprisonment, unemployment, repression, hunger, anything you want. Those are all deaths. And that, that is something else than impurity. Here one would have to ask whether a language game that becomes excessive, that falls into what I was calling *pléonexia*, the "wanting to have too much of it," that is, precisely when such a language game begins to regulate language games that are not the same as itself, isn't such a language game always assisted by the sword?

To be more precise: if a language game owes its efficacy, I would not say only, but also, to the fear of death, even if it is a minority game, it is unjust. Majority does not mean large number, it means great fear. Hence my second question: In order to become a majority, is it necessary to violate the boundaries of the language game concerned?

Isn't there, in the pretension to regulate other language games, something like terror?

JLT: Certainly, but in this way one is talking only about the multiplicity of justices. There remains the justice of multiplicity. . . .

JFL: Yes, there is first a multiplicity of justices, each one of them defined in relation to the rules specific to each game. These rules prescribe what must be done so that a denotative statement, or an interrogative one, or a prescriptive one, etc., is received as such and recognized as "good" in accordance with the criteria of the game to which it belongs. Justice here does not consist merely in the observance of the rules; as in all the games, it consists in working at the limits of what the rules permit, in order to invent new moves, perhaps new rules and therefore new games.

And then the justice of multiplicity: it is assured, paradoxically enough, by a prescriptive of universal value. It prescribes the observance of the singular justice of each game such as it has just been situated: formalism of the rules and imagination in the moves. It authorizes the "violence" that accompanies the work of the imagination. It prohibits terror, that is, the blackmail of death toward one's partners, the blackmail that a prescriptive system does not fail to make use of in order to become the majority in most of the games and over most of their pragmatic positions.

JLT: Here you are talking like the great prescriber himself . . . (laughter).

November 1977-June 1978

Afterword: Literature—Just Making It
by Sam Weber

What I have to say here is inscribed between two *laughs*. They take place on the sixth and seventh day of the week of interviews published under the title *Just Gaming* [*Au juste*].[1] The first laugh intervenes toward the end of a discussion concerning the earlier work of one of the two interlocutors, "JFL," who, it seems, was guilty, in times past, of wanting to construct "a philosophy of the will," in other words, "a monistic philosophy." "It is not worth getting back to it," explains JFL, for it is now clear: "A philosophy of the will cannot be passed, as such, for a political philosophy. It does not work" (90). It does not work because, in a way, it works too well—goes too fast. To take, for example, the dynamics of the death instincts as a model for a politics is in this instance to go too fast, to be in too much of a hurry, for reasons that JFL's interlocutor, "JLT," does not fail to underline: "Any philosophy of the will . . . inevitably gets into matters of velocity (slowdowns, acceleration, sedimentation)." Quite right, responds JFL, that was the case with his interpretation of the death instincts ". . . as acceleration. They are the same as the life instincts, but in a hurry. It is a difference of rhythm." Taking this kind of rhythmic difference as the paradigm of a politics is being in too much of hurry.

This brings us to the first laugh: "JLT: It is a politics that I would call 'American', if you will. JFL (laughter):   Yes, it is quite broadly a politics of capital, actually. That is true. And I think that what interested me, was to see it at work within the capital, to make it appear in its affirmative force. Except that, insofar as one is a political thinker, one cannot do without justice. But the question is: What is this horizon? Which horizon are we determining?"

The least that can be said in response to this capital question is that it would seem that the horizon of justice can be neither that of the will, nor that of velocity (of acceleration, deceleration), nor, finally, that of people in a hurry. None of that can yield more than a politics of capital, an "American" politics. Thus, on the sixth day, the first laugh.

The second would come the next day, the seventh day, definitely a fine Sunday, judging at least by the brevity of the conversation on that day, by far the shortest of the week. This laugh, then, comes right at the end of the book, in which it has, so to speak, the last word. It intervenes after a discussion that attempts, precisely, to delineate this "horizon" of justice, in all its multiplicity. It is a question, *first*, of a multiplicity of justices themselves, each one of which is "defined in relation to the rules specific to each [language] game"; and *then* of a justice "of multiplicity . . . [which] authorizes the 'violence' that accompanies the work of the imagination," while prohibiting the "terror" by which a game, a prescriptive system, attempts to impose itself upon the others, to set itself up as the dominant game, thus reducing the multiplicity to silence. To counter this tendency, to counter this danger that is almost endemic to the agonistic process—the danger of "wanting to have too much of it," the risk of a certain *excess*—it is necessary to assign a referee, put up a safety railing, erect a "singular justice" that sees to it that singularity itself is respected in its irreducible multiplicity.

The response to all of these affirmations is not long in coming, and with it, simultaneously, the end of the book, the end of the week and—the second laugh. JLT is given the last word: "Here you are talking like the great prescriber himself . . . (laughter)."

And, in fact, there is something to laugh about here. For the effort to trace the horizon of justice while avoiding the pitfalls of voluntarism, monism, and velocity—the effort, then, to escape the trap of "American politics"—ends in a "paradox," the contours of which remain extremely difficult to delineate. It is necessary for a singular justice to impose its rule on all the other games, in order that they may retain their own singularity. To safeguard the incommensurability of each game, there must be an authority capable of determining the rules that constitute each game as such, so that afterward the authority can see to it that the integrity of the game is respected and that no one among them imposes itself upon the others. It is thus necessary to be able to distinguish between [*trancher entre*] the violence of the imagination, which produces not only new moves, situated "at the limits of what the rules permit," but also engenders "new rules and therefore new games"—it is necessary to be able to distinguish between this violence, in some way legitimate and necessary, and "terror," described as the attempt to reduce the multiplicity of the games or players through exclusion or domination.

But how, then, can we conceive of such a justice, one that assures, "by a prescriptive of universal value," the *nonuniversality* of singular and incommensurable games? Is it itself a game? Is it singular? These are questions that make us want to laugh, for reasons well analyzed by Freud in his study of jokes. If we laugh at the *Witz*, Freud writes, it is because, "owing to the introduction of the proscribed idea by the route of auditory impressions, the energy of investment used for the inhibition has now become suddenly superfluous and has been lifted, and is therefore now ready to be discharged by laughter."[2] A certain expenditure of energy has thus become superfluous, temporarily, because the representation it tries to inhibit, prohibit, *proscribe*, has imposed itself regardless, "by the route of auditory impressions."

If laughter arises when a forbidden representation succeeds—by a roundabout route, but one that is at the same time that of auditory impressions—in imposing itself despite the inhibition affecting it, one may ask whether, in the laughs we have just described, such a representation is in play, and if so, which one? Let us take a closer look.

One of the convictions that dominates JFL's argument in *Just Gaming* is that there is an irreducible singularity and multiplicity of the different language games. Each game is thought to have its own delimited and delimitable rules, which constitute its determinate singularity. This argumentation is undoubtedly directed against the totalitarian pretensions of totalizing thought. But does not the concept of absolute, intact singularity remain tributary to the same logic of identity that sustains any and all ideas of totality? As soon as we affirm that each game is *absolutely different* from all the others, in theory if not in fact, we are in danger of being caught in the trap we wished to remove from the game. For wanting to determine singularity as the other of the other can only end in the same, in the identical, in the "pure" and the "specific" [*propre*], as Hegel demonstrated very well in relation to the notion of "pure" difference.[3]

In attempting to resist the imperalism of the totalizing perspective, JFL runs the risk of reproducing it as the absolute of an irreducible and incommensurable singularity. The very notion of incommensurability is reminiscent of a certain Marxist critique, which represents commodity production as the quantitative leveling of use-values—which are supposed to be qualitatively incommensurable—by exchange-values (see, for example, the use of the concept of the incommensurable in the writings of Lukács[4]).

A response to this criticism—which seems to have been JFL's during his "American" phase—would be precisely to challenge the opposition "singularity/totality," "incommensurable/equivalent," etc., by pushing the notion of exchange, or of circulation, to the point that it is no longer conceivable within the horizon of the identical or the commensurable. It is at this point that the idea of a "general agonistics" (*The Postmodern Condition*) doubtless becomes indispensable. But as soon as the "field" of such an agonistics is conceived of as being constituted by absolutely incommensurable, and thus essentially determinable, games, the agonistic aspect is paradoxically restricted by that of the *system*—in other words, by the idea of a finite system of rules, without which it would be impossible to conceive of a game being absolute in its singularity. From that moment, struggle is no longer possible outside of a game, but that game as such is not in struggle, and cannot be. For struggle could only be a form of communication with another game, and that, according to *Just Gaming*, is precisely what should not take place. "Here"—that is, in relation to language games—"the Idea of Justice will consist in preserving the purity of each game" and preventing, for example, "denotative or narrative games" from being "infiltrated by prescriptions" (96). That a game like the game of narrative must, necessarily, by its very structure, contain prescriptive moments, that a narration must be imposed upon its listeners, that it must obligate them—none of that seems admissible by the terms of this argument.[5]

Be that as it may, the concern with "preserving the purity" and singularity "of each game" by reinforcing its isolation from the others gives rise to exactly what was intended to be avoided: "the domination of one game by another," namely, the domination of the prescriptive. For without a "great prescriber," no purity, no specificty [*propriété*], no incommensurability, even identified, could be preserved as such.

But if this is the case, it follows that the true function of the great prescriber is not so much to prescribe, but rather to *proscribe*. For if a great prescriber is indispensable, it is primarily in order to proscribe, while at the same time obscuring the necessity for proscription. This great proscriber must see to it that no game plays games with any other. He guards over the multiplicity of the games as if that multiplicity could be delimited without exclusion—while at the same time excluding himself from the field he thus claims to dominate. For the justice of games is not to be toyed with. . . .

This is perhaps the point at which the *Witz* becomes readable. The purity of the singular games can only be affirmed from a position and by an agency that is itself out of bounds, outside the agonistic field; by an agency, therefore, that is entirely *exclusive*, at the same time as it proscribes exclusion as *nonrelation*, as incommensurability. Thus the great proscriber, in determining the multiplicity of the games as the negative effect of the proscribed exclusion, practices precisely what he desires to exclude, to cause to be forgotten. If each game is irreducibly singular, he tells us, it is because it has nothing whatsoever to do with any of the others. It in no way depends on its surroundings, on the other games; relatedness between games is conceived solely in terms of "infiltration," "domination," contamination of their "purity."

We are now beginning to understand why laughter must arise at this point as the articulation of the inarticulable, as the presentation of the unpresentable. By prescribing that no game, especially not that of prescription, should dominate the others, one is doing exactly what it is simultaneously claimed is being avoided: one is dominating the other games in order to protect them from domination. By treating them as singular and incommensurable beings, one is subjecting them, a priori, to determination by another discourse (for no game can be self-determining). In short, the relation to the other is defined in a way that is all the less contestable for being presented as itself out of bounds. The laughter that arises is, perhaps, a witness to the uneasiness of the former player, who has turned referee, but is not yet entirely comfortable with his new role. For as a referee, he must ask himself if, or in what way, he is still in the game. Does the referee play? Or does he only judge? And what if judgment is also a kind of game? If so, how should it be played?

To find an answer to these questions, it is perhaps appropriate to return to a text that *The Postmodern Condition* cites as a basic reference for any theory of a general agonistics. The work in question is by Nietzsche and was published in English under the title "Homer's Contest"[6] (in German: "Homers Wettkampf"; in French, "La joute chez Homer"). As in *Just Gaming*, Nietzsche's argument takes as its point of departure the distinction between two conceptions of struggle: on the one hand, struggle is seen as a means, it is subordinated to a finality determined outside the game (whose goal is thus identified with victory); on the other hand, the game (or struggle) is regarded as an end-in-itself. The first conception finds its most extreme, but also most consequent, expression in what Nietzsche calls the *Vernichtungskampf*, the extermination struggle; the second, in contrast, identified with Greek society during the Homeric epoch, is designated as *agôn* properly speaking, as *Wettkampf* (joust).[7] As we shall see, the fact that these two German terms have the same root—*kampf*: struggle, combat—is not negligible: the terms are different, but not necessarily "incommensurable."

"The core of the Hellenic notion of the joust," writes Nietzsche, is that it "abominates the rule of one (*die Alleinherrschaft*) and fears its dangers; it desires, as a protection against the genius, another genius" (37). At first glance, then, it might seem as though Nietzsche's agonistics and the agonistics elaborated in *Just Gaming* came down to the same thing. However, there is a considerable difference between them. In Nietzsche, the condition of possibility of agonistics is described not as a principle of inclusion—as the singularity proper to each incommensurable game—but as a gesture commonly shared by all of the games, one inseparable from their ludic nature. It is a question of the *ostracism*, the exclusion that makes it possible for the agonistic field to define itself and, especially, to maintain itself—to stay in the game. Those who, by their superiority, would threaten the status of the joust as a game are banished. And if ostracism thus becomes the indispensable condition for the continuation of the joust, it is because the latter is understood from the start as a movement not of identity, but of otherness. The agonistic field, according to Nietzsche, is determined not in relation to the multiplicity of singular games it is supposed to harbor, but rather in relation to an exteriority that is at the same time its own product: the victors. Otherness, then, is not to be sought *between* games that are supposed to be essentially self-identical, but *within* the game as such. This amounts to saying that the game is necessarily *ambivalent* from the start. For its point of departure are feelings of envy, jealousy, and rancor, feelings that, Nietzsche emphasizes, the Greeks experienced not as "a blemish but the gift of a *beneficent* godhead" (35); for they drive one, by a sort of mimetic desire, toward competition with the other —and therefore to the joust. Thus once the game becomes autonomous, it is necessarily self-destructive, for its aim is the elimination of the other upon whom it nevertheless depends. That is why the *Vernichtungskampf*, the extermination struggle, cannot be thought of as simply external to the *Wettkampf*, to the *agôn* properly speaking. What we have, rather, are two sides of a single—ambivalent— dynamic;

this is articulated in a text by Pausanias cited by Nietzsche, in which there are two goddesses who, though different and even in opposition with one another, bear *the same name, Eris* (discord).[8]

Agonistics, then, according to Nietzsche, always contains an element of domination, a desire to lay hold of the other, to curtail the otherness upon which the agonistics nevertheless depends. Agonistics is necessarily ambivalent, and the only question—the question animating Nietzsche's text—concerns the manner in which it tries to assume that ambivalence. The answer given in Nietzsche's text is to show how the Greeks succeeded in recognizing their identity as players as the *effect of an irreducible otherness*. It is only this recognition that can prevent what the Greeks called hybris, which according to Nietzsche consists of the desire to withdraw from the game. Nietzsche describes this recognition as the divinization of otherness:

> Because [the Greek] is envious, he feels equally at each excess
> of honor, wealth, glory, and good fortune the envious eye
> of a god descend upon him, and he fears this envy. . . . But
> this conception in no way turns him away from his gods:
> its extent is on the contrary limited in such a way that human
> beings can *never* have the audacity to risk a joust with
> the gods.[9]

In this relation to the other as god, agonistics recognizes its own limit as irreducible otherness. By regarding himself as a coveted object, the victor avoids the hybris of wishing to stay the same, out of bounds to any game, incommensurable. In contrast, the desire to be without equal was the cause of the fall of Miltiades, the victor at Marathon:

> After the battle of Marathon the envy of the heavenly powers
> seized him. And this divine envy is inflamed when it beholds
> a human being without a rival, unopposed, on a solitary peak of
> fame. Only the gods are beside him now and therefore they
> are against him. They seduce him to a deed of *hybris*
> (excessiveness), and under it he collapses. (38)

When one comes face to face with the other, the other always comes down to the same and the game is already over. It is this thought, in any case, that distinguishes Nietzschean agonistics from that of *Just Gaming*, which dissociates itself from its other, "terror," in a radical way:

> When the group Red Army Fraction makes an incursion and
> destroys the American computer in Heidelberg, that is war; the
> group considers itself at war; it is waging war and it is actually

destroying a part of the forces of the adversary. Very good:
that is part of the rather exact game that is a two-sided war. But
when the same group kidnaps Schleyer and blackmails a third
party with Schleyer's death as the stake, *then we are in altogether different violence that has no relation to the previous
one* and which alone, in my view, deserves the name of
"terrorism." . . . And in such a case, it falls within what I
was just saying: it excludes the game of the just . . .
because the Schleyer in question is obviously taken as a means
here. He is threatened with death, but *this threat is addressed
to a third party, not to him* (67; emphasis added)

Schleyer should be taken for himself, not for another, as a means, addressed to a third party. The third party should be excluded, that is
the game rule, the rule that, according to *Just Gaming*, constitutes—
should constitute—the indispensable condition of all games as such.
This conception of the legitimate game as a "two-sided war" is much
closer to the *Critique of Pure Reason* than to "Homer's Contest," in
which the game is only authorized in relation to this excluded middle
that is the gods, the figure of the otherness at work "within" the
game itself.

This perhaps explains why the discourse that describes the game in
Nietzsche is not, as in *Just Gaming*, in the end "prescriptive"—that is
to say, it is not a discourse that attempts to hide its local determination behind an obligation claiming to come out of nowhere—but
rather *narrative*, in a quite specific sense.[10] For although Nietzsche
describes agonistics as a historical moment framed between two
epochs of unrestrained violence, he does not hesitate to designate
these two epochs as "pre-Homeric." Thus, the agonistics of the
Homeric epoch is not only preceded by a "pre-Homeric" period—
which is not at all surprising—but is also followed by it. This demon-
strates that the temporality of Nietzschean "history" is neither linear
nor irreversible, and that the stability of agonistics is necessarily pre-
carious. For agonistics is determined in relation to a dynamic of ambivalence, such as described by Freud in *Totem and Taboo*:

The instinctual desire [*Die Trieblust*] is constantly shifting in
order to escape from the *impasse* and endeavours to find
substitutes—substitute objects and substitute acts—in place of
the prohibited ones. In consequence of this, the prohibition
itself shifts as well, and extends to any new aims which the forbidden impulse may adopt. Any fresh advance made by the
repressed libido is answered by a fresh sharpening of the prohibition. The mutual inhibition of the two conflicting forces

produces a need for discharge, for reducing the prevailing tension; and to this may be attributed the reason for the performance of compulsive acts [*Zwangshandlungen*]. . . . It is a law of neurotic illness that these compulsive acts fall more and more under the sway of the instinct and approach nearer and nearer to the activity which was originally prohibited.[11]

In this quotation I have taken the liberty of modifying the usual translation of the German word used by Freud, *Zwangshandlungen*; instead of rendering it as "obsessional acts," I have translated it as "compulsive acts," in order to emphasize that the process being described should not be conceived as limited to the field of neurosis. For the constraint, the compulsion, the *Zwang* in question, is at work everywhere desire comes into conflict with itself, everywhere, therefore, an act, object, or place is simultaneously coveted and repelled. The resultant displacements mark the fitful rhythm of a game that can no longer be entirely localized or determined, since it is constantly dislocating itself. The field traversed by such a game no longer possesses the stability of an intact interior, nor the purity of an incommensurable singularity, such as the following quote from *Just Gaming* seems to attribute to it: "And in each instance, one is in a game, a game with rules, and I play with these rules in order to achieve some effects upon the one I am playing with" (54). In contrast, the game described by Freud under the name *ambivalence* displaces itself in such a way that it prevents one from ever entirely entering into it. To play the unconscious, then, is always to cheat. For one cannot be "in" a game that never ceases to displace itself, to modify its prohibitions, and therefore its rules. The "rule" of such a game is that one is always "out of bounds" [*hors-jeu*], always in violation of the determined and determinable rules; and what is more, that the very determination of these rules implies their violation.[12]

It follows that each determination, each definition of the game can only be accomplished as a more or less provisory, more or less violent *arresting* [*arrêt*: stopping; court decision, sentence] of a dynamic that is interminable, but never simply indeterminate or infinite. For a dynamic such as this can only be conceived as a series of highly conflictual determinations, as a movement of ambivalence, in which the other is always being seized as a function of the same, all the while eluding this capture. The other becomes the intimate condition of possibility of the game, remaining all the while out of bounds, like the gods.

It is for this reason that the game of ambivalence in Freud cannot be understood in terms of the binary logic that so often—but not always, as we shall see—determines the agonistic horizon in *Just Gaming*, as demonstrated in the following paragraph, which is precisely about Freud:

> A dream . . . : it is a language game that Freud has described fairly well, with its own logic or its own rhetoric. It is a statement that positions the utterer as an unknown utterer and the addressee as the ordinary utterer of wakeful discourses, that is, as the dreamer himself. (52; translation modified)

But if Freud described the dream fairly well and did indeed describe it as a language game, it was, was it not, a matter of a game: not of a *statement* [*énoncé*], but of an utterance [*énonciation*], what Freud called a "form of thought," the distinctive characteristic of which, according to him, was to *distort—enstellen—*that same thought, in other words, to distort thought insofar as it is an articulation of the same, of meaning.

It is this function of the dream as *Entstellung* that forbids us, should forbid us, from describing the dream as a game that "positions" its subjects according to determinate posts (such as "utterer"/ "addressee"). For if the dream in Freud is in point of fact a game, "bound to a precise pragmatics" (52; translation modified), the most remarkable effect of that pragmatics is to make a certain *imprecision* ineradicable. The principal operation of the dream is less to "position" than to "un-position" every post one may assume, which in the final analysis should prevent us from speaking, with rigor, of the "dreamer *himself.*" For it is rather the Same as such that is *part* of the dream, without, however, the dream becoming a *whole.*

If the dream can be described as a game, it is not simply because it has "an effect upon the world," but rather, because it is articulated as a struggle, as a conflict whose resolution can only be provisory and partial. And this resolution always implies a narrative. That is why the "pragmatics" of the dream is reminiscent of that of the "narration of popular tale" as analyzed in *Just Gaming* (and also in *The Postmodern Condition*). According to this analysis, the privileged term in these tales is the narrated, not as a content, but as an interminable and indeterminable "relaying." For every effort to determine it becomes itself a variation and continuation of the story. Thus it can be said that "we are always immanent to stories in the making, even when we are the ones telling the story to the other"(43).

But if this analysis of the "pagan" pragmatics of popular narratives appears fairly close to that recounted by Freud in relation to the dream, this very proximity brings out quite clearly the difference between the two stories. For in Freud we can never be in a position that is totally "immanent" to the stories we tell because—here as elsewhere—the stories are not "immanent" to themselves. They are always in the process of going elsewhere, in the sense of *Entstellung*, and it is this movement—caught in the double requirement on the one hand to displace itself and on the other hand to arrest its movement [*s'arrêter*], to take a fixed position—that marks the unconscious agonistics as ambivalent.[13] That is why, in the Freudian perspective, we cannnot be entirely "in" a game or story, any more than we can be squarely "outside" the stories we tell. But if, in dreams as in popular narratives, "there is no place one can go to photograph the whole scene," it is not because, as we read in *Just Gaming*, "there is no exteriority," but because in a certain sense, there is only that; as soon as the unconscious is in play, we are dealing with an exteriority that tries to exclude itself, in other words to internalize, incorporate, appropriate itself, without ever managing to do it. But if we can never succeed in this impossible effort, neither can we renounce it, and it is precisely this double impossibility that makes the game of the unconscious both imprecise (because it is never completely determinable) and ambivalent (because it is always in the process of arresting itself, of revolving around a "fixation").

This shows why the game of the unconscious does not proceed by "moves" [*coups*], but by post-factos [*après-coups*], or again, by fits and starts [*à-coups*]. The fits and starts of the unconscious always come too early or too late, or both at the same time. Which is to say that they . . . *just* make it [*arrivent . . . de justesse*]. At least, that is what the beginning of the last chapter of *The Interpretation of Dreams* indicates in a context that is entirely agonistic, to the extent that Freud attempts to defend his analyses against anticipated objections, against a critique that creates a "danger that the very thing whose value we have undertaken to assess may slip completely through our fingers."[14] It is a question of defining the exact manner in which the dream is transmitted, particularly in relation to the inevitable "forgetting" to which it is submitted. This question brings into focus the fundamental problem of the status of the dream insofar as it can be deformed—*entstellt*—by its post-facto narration.

> It is true that we distort dreams in attempting to reproduce
> them; here we find at work once more the process that we have
> described as the secondary (and often ill-conceived) revision
> of the dream by the agency that carries on normal thinking. But
> this distortion is itself no more than a part of the revision
> to which the dream-thoughts are regularly subjected as a result
> of dream censorship.[15]

But this deformation, Freud insists, is only the "part of dream-distortion that operates manifestly"; "a much more far-reaching process of distortion, though a less obvious one, has already developed the dream out of the hidden dream-thoughts."[16]

Thus the dream as *Entstellung*—and with the dream, all the (de) formations of the unconscious—are always already constructed according to a pragmatics that assumes here a *proleptic* form. Thus the dream, in general, faced with censorship, behaves in the same way as Freud, whose actions are a function of anticipated objections. What distinguishes the distortions of the unconscious is that they endeavor to hide their own operation of distortion (in German, one would say that it is a question of *sich vertellenden Entstellungen*).

But if the dream must be considered as a prior distortion of this kind, unarrested and unfixed in an ambivalent, agonistic game, then the danger Freud seems to attribute to a certain exterior—his (more or less malicious) readers—already dwells within: in an "object" that cannot "slip through our fingers" for the simple reason that it is not a veritable *object*, but rather a stake in a highly conflictual dynamic, one we may also designate *interpretation*. For interpretation, like narration, is not simply external to the dream, it is an active participant in the dream itself (while still distorting it). The dream thus becomes inseparable from a process of interpretation that in turn implies a play (and a relation) of force:

> The question whether it is possible to interpret *every* dream
> must be answered in the negative. It must not be forgotten that
> in interpreting a dream we are opposed by the psychical forces
> that were responsible for its distortion. It is thus a question
> of relative strength whether our intellectual interest, our
> capacity for self-transcension [*die Fähigkeit zur Selbstüber-
> windung*], our psychological knowledge, and our practice
> in interpreting dreams enables us to master our internal
> resistances. It is always possible to go *some* distance.[17]

The whole problem is there—there in Freud's text, though not necessarily in the translations. For the French translation, otherwise admirable, seems to me to follow the Standard Edition in rendering the German phrase, "die Fähigkeit zur Selbstüberwindung," as "self-mastery,"[18] This translation could itself be described as a case of secondary revision. Although the interpreter must try to "surmount himself," to transcend himself, there can never be any question of his attaining "self-mastery," which would be just the opposite of what is necessary to interpret dreams. For such mastery could only reflect the agency it is necessary to surmount, *überwinden*: the ego (which Freud identifies here with the *Self*, the *Selbst*). The point of view of the ego, of self-mastery, can be none other than that found in the secondary revision of the dream, which it therefore remains constitutionally incapable of interpreting.

Although the interpreter must endeavor to transcend the self, this attempt can never fully succeed, it can only go *"some* distance," for the attempt cannot go without what it is attempting to go beyond: the strength of the ego. It is thus necessary to "master our internal resistances" using the very same forces that contribute to those resistances: that is the paradox permeating psychoanalysis, the paradox that explains why it is appropriate to describe all of its games—whether it is a question of dreams, the *Witz*, "free" association, transference, etc.—as *ambivalent*.

In contrast to a theory of agonistics as a multiplicity of absolutely singular, incommensurable, and noncommunicating games, Nietzsche's conceptions lead us to ask whether is it not rather ambivalence—in other words, a certain *tension* between unity and disunity—that characterizes all games as such. This does not mean making ambivalence a new transcendental or totalizing principle, for while it signals that a certain will to totality, mastery, power is perhaps untranscendable, it reminds us of the impossibility of such a will ever imposing itself once and for all. On the other hand, proscribing this ambivalence in the name of purity and singularity of each game in itself almost always means putting what is proscribed into action. For example, the insistence with which, in *Just Gaming*, it is constantly stated that the various games are "incommunicable to each other," that "justice" would consist in "preserving the purity of each game," thus in protecting them from "infiltrations" supposedly coming in from outside —all of these gestures resemble the "compromise formations" by means of which a desire undertakes to bypass the prohibitions blocking it. A proscribed desire to touch, for example, can succeed in imposing itself by claiming to keep things apart, to be preventing them from becoming entangled, from rubbing up against one another. Touching everything and everybody, so that nothing will touch. Allowing laughter, but only parenthetically.

How can we judge if we are already, still, always, caught in a game in which the moves [*coups*] come only in fits and starts, post facto [*à-coup, après-coup*], hurried yet late at the same time? How can we judge if space and time, if the place of judgment, is wracked by ambivalence, if every attempt to cut to the heart of the matter [*trancher*: cut; contrast; conclude] necessarily involves an attempt to retrench [*retrancher*], and also to be entrenched [*se retrancher*] in, behind, and around the slices [*tranches*] thus cut [*coupées*]. How can we judge, if not by . . . cutting it close [. . . *de justesse*].

Just making it is not necessarily the same as making it just [*de justesse* vs. *justice*]. Obviously, it all depends on the multiplicity in play, on the singularity of the utterers, of the addressees, and perhaps also on where it all takes place. If it takes place in France, in Normandy for example, it can only be a question of "justice," which, consigned to the auditory route—for we are still between two laughs—is heard as ʒystis. If, on the other hand, it takes place somewhere else, in the United States for example, then it can only be a question of something pronounced like this, dʒʌstis, and written *justice*. But if we take a "hybrid" case, for example, that of an American who has recently displaced himself from his discursive universe and is attempting to find a compromise between what he believes he knows under the name "justice" (dʒʌstis) and what he believes he knows, less well, under the name "justice" (ʒystis), then he will not fail to find, halfway between the two words, something that, while resembling both, is not exactly either one; that is, he will find his compromise, *de justesse*.

It is of this compromise, of [*de*] *justesse* that I would like to speak in the small amount of space I have left. Of *justesse*, then, not as such, not as a "quality that permits one to execute a thing very exactly," nor as a "quality that makes a thing perfectly adapted or appropriate to its purpose" (*Le Petit Robert*). Rather, I would like to speak of *justesse* in its adverbial usage, as for example when we designate the manner in which an event, an act, a thing can almost not make it, or the way in which something has a hard time making it [*a de la peine à arriver*], hardly makes it [*arrivant à peine*]. You see, it is a question of something that just manages to make it [*qui réussit tout juste à arriver*], perhaps because it was cut a little close [*calculé un peu juste*], or because there were obstacles to overcome, barriers to get by, resistances to surmount. As in a sporting contest, or in a fight, where one can win (or lose) just by a hair [*de justesse*]. Or like an accident, which may have been just avoided [*de justesse*]. Or finally, like a text that manages to be written, but just [*qui ne réussit à s'écrire que de justesse*].

Would a text of this kind—supposing that such a thing is possible, or at least thinkable—still deserve to be designated *literature*? In short, can we speak of a literature, not of justice, but—*de justesse*?

As there is not enough time for me to discuss, or even explain, these questions, unavoidable as they are, I will rush straight to a text that can eventually provide us with the elements of a response. The text in question is a narrative by Kafka known in French under the title "Le Verdict." This title, in German "Das Urteil," presents us with a characteristic problem in translating Kafka, described by Marthe Robert as follows:

> The simplest words are those surest to be betrayed, because the equivalents have neither the same age, the same degree of condensation, nor the same ambiguity. Though there is no other word to translate the original, our "trial," confined as it is to the juridical sphere, cannot fully play its role.[19]

The word "verdict," in remaining, like "trial," limited to the juridical sphere, only continues a story already begun by that other word capable of translating *Urteil*: "judgment" (the choice of the English translators). This word, as you know, comes from *jus-dicere*, thus from "right" or "law," inasmuch as it is bound to an act of discourse. The German word, on the other hand, takes us into an entirely different sphere, that of economics, exchange, and circulation, "lending, borrowing, and debt" (Benveniste).[20] Thus if "judgment," and "verdict" to an even greater extent, is located *within* a juridical space already constituted, organized, and polarized by the oppositions between true and false, right and wrong, innocent and guilty, then the word *Urteil* remains much closer to the move itself by which we parcel out (*er-teilen*) or divide up space as such. *Urteil* thus brings us to something that is not yet totally articulated, not yet separated, opposed, or singularized, to a certain *informity* [*informité*] or, why not?, to a certain *infirmity* — like the one that seems to affect the father in Kafka's narrative.

But before going into the details, or at least into a few of the details, I will summarize the story; this will inevitably distort it (that is the law of the genre), but it will perhaps serve as a reminder of what is at issue nevertheless. It all happens one fine Sunday morning. Georg Bendemann is writing a letter to a friend from his youth, who left the country years back to set up as a merchant in St. Petersburg. The letter proves difficult to write, because the two friends' fortunes have gone in totally opposite directions. While the friend in St. Petersburg seems to have been a failure both in his business and in his personal life, Georg, for his part, has had nothing but success. The family business is quickly growing, and Georg is preparing to marry "a girl from a well-to-do family" (79).[21] Despite a certain reluctance because of the disparity between their two lives, Georg decides to announce the news of his marriage to his less fortunate friend and invite him to come to the wedding. After finishing the letter, Georg goes to his father's room to tell him of his decision to stop hiding things from his friend. Georg is quite surprised by the air of decrepitude surrounding his father and is even more disconcerted when it appears that his father has no memory whatsoever of his friend. Georg reproaches himself for having neglected his father's condition, and he resolves to help him find a life-style more suited to his advanced age. This resolution is strengthened when he fails to bring back his father's memory of his friend; when his father starts to deny that the friend ever existed, the son suggests that he go to bed to get some rest. He carries him to bed in his arms, helps him undress and get in, and pulls the covers over his father, who seems to behave like a child while all this is going on. But as soon as the father is settled in bed, "well covered up" by his son's solicitude, he suddenly [*tout d'un coup*] sits up in bed—the father's move [*coup*]—and begins to revile his son: "You have disgraced your mother's memory, betrayed your friend, and stuck your father into bed so that he can't move. But he can move, or can't he?" (85). Georg is reproached for having betrayed those closest him, especially on account of the woman he wants to marry. But, the father insists, everyone has caught on to Georg's betrayals, everyone, of course, but Georg himself, who only had eyes for the object of his desires: "because she lifted up her skirts like this and this . . ." (85). And then comes the moment when Georg also must *know*—the moment of the *Urteil*:

> So now you know what else there is in the world besides yourself, till now you've known only about yourself! An innocent child, yes, that you were, at bottom, but still more fundamentally have you been a diabolical being!—And therefore take note: I sentence you to death by drowning! (87)

All there is left to do is carry out the punishment, execute the *Uretil*, which Georg does with the greatest of zeal, at high speed, jumping into the river from a bridge across from the house.

So that is the story, recounted, distorted, dislocated—and above all, divested of nearly all of the course-altering details that give it its power of fascination. But I must hurry, for the time that has been kindly accorded me for these comments is long over (has it been over forever?)—and therefore I will get straight to what I find striking in this narrative: it is not so much the outlandish "verdict" of the father, but rather the alacrity with which it is put into action by the person it targets. If this speed is surprising, it is doubtless because it forces us to question everything that, in the first reading, seemed to be self-evident, to go without saying. Let us start with Georg's position, and that of the narrator, who seems to be quite close to his hero. The father's verdict, and the zeal with which it is executed by the son, takes away our confidence that we are dealing with a discourse we can trust. All of a sudden [*d'un coup*], the temporal hierarchy—of the narrated, the narrating agency, and the "lectant" (the reader reading)—is no longer fixed or reliable. If Georg rushes off to carry out his father's *Urteil*, without a word of protest, is that not a sign that what just happened was perhaps already there, had been for a long time—maybe forever?—that the game had already been played out before the players arrived, before the moves [*coups*] had fallen. But that everything was already there, in its place, had been for a long time, does not mean that it is possible to locate that place. It is perhaps so close to us that we can barely succeed in finding a footing there. We find ourselves in the same position Georg is in when he tries, for the last time, to defend himself against his father:

> "So you've been lying in wait for me?" cried Georg. His father said pityingly, in an offhand manner: "Suppose you wanted to say that sooner. But now it is no longer appropriate." (87)

Everything is thus in its proper place, everything—but us. That is the *Witz* of the story. But along with us, everything else is also displaced, begins to totter, and perhaps to fall. That is at least what Georg hopes for when confronted by his father:

> Now he'll lean forward, thought Georg, what if he topples and smashes himself! These words went hissing through his mind. His father leaned forward but did not topple. Since Georg did not come any nearer, as he had expected, he straightened himself again. (86)

Mr. Bendemann the elder leans but does not fall—not yet, at any rate. (In English one might translate it, he "bends, but does not break"). Therefore, it is up to Georg to fall, which he does with all speed, with relief it would seem, almost with enthusiasm.

But who, or what, is Georg? What is signified by this proper name? A son, undoubtedly, but a son who also plays the role of the mother and the father, whom he undresses and carries to bed in his arms. "Georg" is also the name of a being who, according to his father, was, at bottom, "an innocent child, but still more fundamentally . . . a diabolical being." So what kind of being is *fundamentally* both *innocent* and *diabolical*? What is this bottom ground that harbors such contradictory qualities? Can we ever hope to plumb its depths, or at least have it safely and directly in view? For that is also tied to the name, "Georg":

> Georg shrank into a corner, as far away from his father as
> possible. A long time ago he had firmly made up his mind to
> watch closely every last movement so that he should not
> be surprised by any indirect attack, a pounce from behind or
> above. At this moment he recalled this long-forgotten resolve
> and forgot it again, like a man drawing a short thread
> through the eye of a needle. (85)

"Georg" is also the end of the Cartesian cogito, of the subject as self-consciousness, for between *self* and *consciousness*, there is the *forgetting* that accompanies each act of thought like its indissociable shadow. More space, more time to back away to "observe," sheltered from any unwelcome surprise from "behind or above." "Georg" is also the game of *da/fort* ["here/gone"], in which no mastery is possible any longer, in which one can only lose the thread one draws. One never stops passing beyond, without being able to say where one has been.

Thus it is that the proper name "Georg" becomes the stake in another space and time, wracked by ambivalence, where innocence and the diabolical, memory and forgetting, love and hate shake hands, rub against one another, infiltrate each other. Confronted by such a spectacle, it becomes impossible to distinguish what *should have* remained separate: terror and violence, riot and revolution, remorse and desire:

> Georg stared at that bogey conjured up by his father. His friend
> in St. Petersburg, whom his father suddenly knew too well,
> touched his imagination as never before. Lost in the vastness of
> Russia he saw him. Among the wreckage of his showcases,
> the slashed remnants of his wares, the falling gas brackets, he
> was just standing up. Why did he have to go so far away! (85)

This vision—which is *also* that of the fall of the house of Bendemann—fixes upon the last remaining landmark, the friend, who, with everything falling down, manages, in a manner, to stand. But it is the manner that counts, and in the English and French translations, it loses what, in *Just Gaming* and *The Postmodern Condition*, is described as the singular rhythm of popular tales, that "beating in place," "immemorial beating" that is sustained by forgetting rather than memory (or rather, is sustained by their complicity and tension).

In the German text, the figure that Georg sees does not allow himself to be located once and for all: "Zwischen den Trümmern der Regale, den zerfetzen Waren, den fallenden Gasarmen stand er gerade noch" [Among the wreckage of his showcases, the slashed remnants of his wares, the falling gas brackets, he was just standing up"]. After the three beats [*coups*] of all that is falling, it is the moment of the subject, the "friend." But "he" does both more and less than the French translation says (which has him "encore debout," 110, where the English has him "just standing up"): he is standing . . . cutting it close [*de justesse*]; and he is hardly [*à peine*] up: *gerade noch*. He is not "encore debout" ["still standing"], but rather: "toujours debout" ["always/still standing"]. Before the bogey of his father, he is hardly up, at the limit, cutting it close.

"Georg" is what is no longer holding up. He is "already gone," "the crash with which is father fell on the bed behind him . . . still in his ears" (87); "already he was grasping the railings as a starving man clutches food. . . . With weakening grip he was still holding on," then let himself fall (88). "Into the void," the French translation tells us (114) — as if to fill in something that would be even more upsetting than this "void," which at least can be given a name. The German text, however, knows nothing of this void (". . . und ließ sich hinabfallen"). There is nothing here to plug the gap, if the bridge itself does not do so, or rather what just arrives on it *at that moment*: "At this moment a quite endless stream of traffic (*eine geradezu unendliche Verkehr*) was just going over the bridge." In the French translation, we read: "a literally mad stream of traffic" (115). And it is in fact a question of something approaching madness: a stream of traffic that is "absolutely endless," that no longer wants to end and thus, at that moment, infiltrates the fall, preventing it from being totally complete. The moment explodes, like a burst of laughter or sobbing. In the twinkling of an eye, "in diesem Augenblick," there comes a "stream of traffic" [*une circulation* in French] that can no longer stop [*s'arrêter*], not even in what is called its own, literal meaning [*son sense dit propre*]. For in German, it is a question not of the word "traffic" or "circulation," but of *Verkehr*. It is the last word of the narrative, and what it suggests is that the story has only begun. *Verkehr* is also transportation, commerce, contact, the sexual act (but curiously, in German, the sexual act is designated less as an act as a *relation*). The German word, then, does more than *signify* the circulation of traffic, it enters circulation itself, it starts to circulate, and the relations it makes audible become "absolutely" interminable, *geradezu unendlich*.

So perhaps there remains nothing for us to do but to judge, to play, to cut to the heart of the matter, to try to arrest the machine in motion, at least for a moment, for a twinkling of an eye, just long enough for a fitful start, judging, as always . . . *de justesse.*

Notes

1. References to this book will be given in parentheses in the text.

2. Sigmund Freud, *Jokes in Their Relation to the Unconscious*, in the *Standard Edition of the Works of Sigmund Freud*, trans. James Strachey (London: The Hogarth Press, 1960), vol. 8, p. 149. Most of the German citations have, as is the case here, been modified, to a greater or lesser degree, in relation to the English translations given as the reference.

3. Hegel, *The Science of Logic*, vol. II, pt. 1, ch. 2, B. 1, "Absolute Difference" (*Der absolute Unterschied*).

4. See, for example, György Lukács, *Balzac und der französische Realismus* (Berlin: Aufbau-Verlag, 1952).

5. Thus, although it is admitted that "one can play simultaneously several games . . . this is nearly always the case," it is insisted that "nonetheless, in principle it is always determinable, by means of the nature of the forms of the statements and by their own efficiences" (*Just Gaming*, p. 54). It is just this *determinability* that this text seeks to challenge.

6. *The Portable Nietzsche*, ed. and trans. Walter Kaufmann, abridged version (New York: Viking, 1968), pp. 32-39.

7. For the translation of *Wettkampf* as *joust* (in French, *joute*), see Friedrich Nietzsche, *Oeuvres complètes, Ecrits posthumes 1870-1873* (Paris: Gallimard, 1975), pp. 374-75. In the quotes from the English translation given here, "contest" has been changed to "joust."

8. If I am not mistaken, the theme of the *proper name* as the locus and operator of conflict and play, as elaborated here in this text in relation to Nietzsche, and below in relation to Kafka, finds theoretical confirmation in a study by Lyotard. It remains to be seen to what extent this theory of the proper name is compatible with the conception of incommensurable language games.

9. This passage was omitted from the English translation.

10. Thus, the narrative game can be a form by which one assumes a relation to otherness, without, however, claiming to have appropriated it.

11. Sigmund Freud, *Totem and Taboo*, in *Standard Edition*, vol. 13, p. 30.

12. This gives Freudian thought itself, and not only the "objects" it theorizes, an ambivalent and highly unstable agonistic character, which I have attempted to analyze elsewhere.

13. For the different resonances of the word *arrêt*, see Jacques Derrida, "Living On," *Deconstruction and Criticism* (New York: The Seabury Press, 1979), and Samuel Weber, "Closure and Exclusion," *Diacritics* 10, no. 2 (Summer 1980): 35-46.

14. Sigmund Freud, *The Interpretation of Dreams*, in *Standard Edition*, vol. 5, pp. 512-13.

15. Ibid., p. 514.

16. Ibid.

17. Ibid., pp. 524-25.

18. Sigmund Freud, *L'interprétation des rêves* (Paris: PUF, 1980), p. 436. The French rendering is "maîtrise de soi": the *Standard Edition* has "self-discipline."

19. Marthe Robert, *As Lonely as Franz Kafka*, trans. Ralph Mannheim (New York: Harcourt, Brace, Jovanovich, 1982), p. 234. Translation modified.

20. Emile Benveniste, *Indo-European Language and Society*, trans. Elizabeth Palmer (London: Faber, 1973), pp. 145-58 (for *Urteil*), and pp. 389-98 (for "judgment").

21. Franz Kafka, "The Judgment," in *The Metamorphosis*, trans. Willa and Edwin Muir (New York: Schocken, 1972). References to this story are given in parentheses in the text.

Index

Index

Abraham, 64
Addressee, 5, 6, 10, 12, 16n, 23-24, 30, 31, 32, 33, 49, 52, 54, 57, 58, 110; occulted, 9, 37, 71-72; privileging of, 36, 37-38. *See also* Audience, Meta-addressee, Narrattee, Reader
Adiaphorai, 48
Agón, 106
Agonistics, 81, 102; general, 104-5; in Freud, 108-13; in Nietzsche, 106-7
Algeria, 69-70
Als Ob, 77-78
Ambivalence, 106-7, 108-10, 111, 113-14, 118
D'Ans, André Marcel, 32-35
Anticipation, 112; of opinion, 79
Antinomy, 58, 80, 82
Antiphonius, 77
Antisthenes, 15
Apophantikos, 22
Ariston, 48-49, 59
Aristotle, 4, 24, 30, 38, 64, 73; on judgment, 14, 26, 43, 47, 59, 78-80, 82, 88; on justice, 26-29; on opinion, 57-58, 59, 74, 75, 95; and paganism, 27-28, 29; *De interpretatione*, 21-22; *Nicomachean Ethics*, 26, 28; *Politics*, 28; *Rhetoric*, 26, 28, 78-80; *Topics*, 28

Arresting (*arrêt*), 109, 111, 120n13
Art, 28, 33, 50, 51, 61-62, 71; vanguard in, 10
Artifice, 8
"As if," 77-78
Atheism, 36
Aubenque, Pierre, 29
Audience: for pop music, 12-13; for writing, 8-11
Aufklärung (Enlightenment), 11, 64, 76
Augustine, Saint, 15
Author, 3-9, 14, 36; of the law, 31, 35. *See also* Sender
Autonomy, 24, 25, 29-32, 33, 34, 36, 37, 38
Autonomy movements, 31

Baader-Meinhof group, 68
Barthes, Roland, 10
Benveniste, Emile, 115
Binarism, 109-10
Bonapartism, 91
Boundaries, 42-43
Buback, Siegfried, 68
Buber, Martin, 91, 97
Butor, Michel, 8-9

Cage, John, 34

Capital, 90, 101-2
Cashinahua, narrative practices of, 32-35, 39, 41
Casuistry, 88
Causality, 65, 70, 87
Charles, Daniel, 34
Christianity, 63, 69; God in, 39-43, 46
Circulation, 104, 119
Citation, 45, 49
Classicism: role of author, 9-11; role of reader, 12; will in, 18
Clastres, Pierre, 41
Cogito, 29-30, 36, 38, 118
Command, 22, 24, 64-65
Communication, 10-11, 54, 104
Compromise formations, 113
Compulsion, 109
Conatus, 48
Concept: and history, 15; maximization of, 46, 47, 58, 75, 77-78, 80
Conformity, to law, 65
Congruence, 94-95
Conjuncture, 56
Consciousness, 118
Consensus, 15, 81
Constative, 49
Constitutions, 21, 25, 27, 28, 95
Content, 5, 6, 18, 34, 83, 86, 91, 92, 99. *See also* Real, Referent
Context, 54-57
Conventionalism, 64, 74, 77, 81
Corax, 78-80
Corneille, Pierre, 9, 16
Criteria. *See* Judgment, criteria of
Custom, 75, 79, 95
Cynics, 74

Death, 99-100
Death Instinct, 90, 101
Democracy, 25, 92
Denomination, 58
Denotation (description), 18, 20-22, 26, 29, 30, 37, 49, 51, 85, 86, 96. *See also* Prescription, derived from denotation
Descartes, René, 18, 24, 30, 118
Description. *See* Denotation
Desire, 48, 108
Determination, 54, 84-85, 87, 91-92, 105, 108, 109, 120n5; local, 108
Détienne, Marcel, 16
Diachrony, 93

Diderot, Denis, 11-12
Difference, 33, 90; pure, 103
Discord, 107
Discourse: aesthetic, 16, 90; apophantic, 22, 24-25; dialectical, 4, 24, 26, 27, 28, 29, 59, 79, 80; dialogic, 4-5, 56-57; didactic, 24, 26, 29, 50; fictional, 5-6; genres of, 24; ideological, 69; literary, 4-5, 10, 12, 49, 50, 52, 114; metaphysical, 44-47, 49, 64, 77, 85, 88; ontological, 22, 29, 44, 53-54, 59, 60, 64, 65, 66; pedagogical, 4, 26, 67; poetic, 4, 5, 24, 33, 36, 51; rhetorical, 4, 24, 79, 83; rhythm in, 34-35; scientific, 24, 28, 29, 30-31, 37, 51, 81; theoretical, 5, 10, 19-29. *See also* Language games, Pragmatics
Dissoi Logoi ("Two Discourses"), 80
Distortion, in the unconscious, 110, 111-12
Distribution, 9, 19, 20, 21, 22-23, 29
Doctrine, 62
Dreams, 36, 52, 110-13
Dufrenne, Mikel, 90
Dvořák, Antonin, 13

Ego, 113
Eikos, 76
Enlightenment, 11, 64, 76
Entstellung, 110, 111-12
Enunciation (utterance), 29-30, 110
Epistémè, 21, 26, 27
Eris, 107
Eristics, 81
Essence, 18, 19
Ethics, 16, 49, 60, 64, 73-74, 88, 89
Ethnology, 38
Ethos, 26, 27
Euchè, 22, 23
Excess, 97, 99, 102, 107
Exchange-value, 104
Exclusion, 66-68, 105, 106
Experimentation, 9-10, 12, 14, 34, 49
Exteriority, 111

Fashion, 9
Film, 61
Finality, 47, 48, 65, 71, 76, 77, 80-81, 94-95
Fixation, 111
Forgetting, 33, 34, 37-38, 118
Free association, 113
Freedom, 23-24, 30, 35, 37, 46, 70, 84-85, 91

French Revolution, 91, 97-98
Freud, 48, 49, 52, 62, 103; agonistics in, 108-13; on dreams, 110-13; *Beyond the Pleasure Principle*, 90; *The Interpretation of Dreams*, 111; *Totem and Taboo*, 108-9
Games, 103, 106
God: in Christianity, 39-43, 46; in Judaism, 22, 38, 52
Gods, pagan, 17, 40-41, 42-45, 107
Good, 100
Grimm, Jakob, 13
Guayaki Indians, 41

Hassidism, 65, 66, 91-92, 97-98
Héxis, 26
Hegel, G. W. R., 12, 37, 53, 69, 89; *Principles of the Philosophy of Right*, 30, 77
Heim, 42
Heteronomy, 32, 35-38
History, 10, 14-15, 18, 34, 53, 108; reason of, 73, 74
Homer, 39-40
Horizon, 77, 82-83, 86, 91, 102
Humanism, 21
Hume, David, 87
Humor, 12, 65, 98, 99
Hybris, 107

Idea, 8, 23, 27, 59, 65, 83, 91, 93, 97; of human society, 58, 85; of justice, 96-97; in Kant, 46-47, 49, 59, 70-71, 74-78, 88; politics of, 95; of totality, 86-88
Ideality, 80
Identity, 33, 103, 106
Illocution, 37
Imagination, 17-18, 61, 62, 78, 100, 102, 103
Immanence, 43, 48, 72, 110-11
Immorality, 70
"In such a way that," 47
Indifferentism, 48
Inhibition, 103, 108-9
Injustice, 65-68, 90
Innovation, 14
Institution, 23
Instruction, 55-59
Intelligentsia, 24, 56, 59, 74
Intensity, 90
Interpretation, 112-13
Irony, 12, 14

Jacobinism, 75, 91-92, 97-98
Joke (*Witz*), 103, 105, 113, 117
Joust, 106
Joyce, James, 50
Judaism: God in, 22, 38, 52; on justice, 52-53, 97; prescription (obligation) in, 17, 30, 37-39, 41-42, 63-64, 65-66. *See also* Hassidism
Judgment: aesthetic, 90; case by case, 27, 28-29, 47, 56, 73-74, 86; 99; criteria of, 14-16, 17, 18, 19, 26, 27, 43, 68, 82, 98; faculty of, 88; as imagining of effects, 65, 67; in Kant, 17, 48, 82; motivation for, 48; politics of, 8; reflective, 75, 76, 77, 85, 87-88; synthetic, 79; and *Uretil*, 115-17
Justesse, 114
Justice: in Aristotle, 26-29; based on opinion, 76; and denotation, 20-22; horizon of, 82-83; Idea of, 96-97; in Judaism, 52-53, 97; and judgment ability, 17; and *justesse*, 114; and modernity, 29-30; in Plato, 19-21, 22-23; and plurality, 95-100, 102; and prescription, 25; as purity of language games, 96; and sender, 71-72; and transcendence, 69-70; and truth, 23-24

Kafka, Franz: "The Judgment," 115-19, 120n8
Kant, Immanuel, 33, 44-45, 69, 77, 96, 99; on concept, 58; and democracy, 92; on finality, 94; on freedom, 84; on Idea, 31, 46-47, 49, 58, 59, 70-71, 74-78; on judgment, 17, 48, 82; on opinion, 79-83; postulates in, 45-46, 47; prescription in, 85-86; on totality, 87-88, 93; on transcendence, 71; on will, 87; *Critique of Judgment*, 15, 18, 48, 73, 75, 80, 81, 86, 88, 91; *Critique of Practical Reason*, 17, 30, 45, 48, 80, 86 88; *Critique of Pure Reason*, 73, 80, 81, 108; *Idea of a History from a Cosmo-Political Point of View*, 76, 86; "Project for a Perpetual Peace," 64, 86; "Theory and Practice," 76; "What is Enlightenment?" 76
Knowledge, 26, 28, 59, 73, 75, 83, 86, 87, 91, 97

Lacan, Jacques, 89
Language. *See* Discourse, Language games, Metalanguage, Speech

Language games, 7, 17, 49; efficacy of, 4, 51-52, 54, 57, 61, 62, 110; exclusion of players, 66-68; incommensurability of, 22, 50-51, 58, 94, 102-5, 113, 120n8; invention of moves, 61-62, 100, 103; plurality of, 49-50, 54, 58-61, 93-100, 102, 106; purity (singularity) of, 64, 96-97, 99, 102-5, 113; rules of, 54, 62, 72, 109; translatability of, 53. *See also* Addressee, Content, Context, Constative, Denotation, Discourse, Illocution, Message, Narrative, Narrattee, Performative, Prescription, Referent, Sender, Statements, Writing
Laughter, 101, 102, 103, 105
Law, 21, 30, 32, 52, 64, 65, 84, 91, 99; author of, 31, 35, 64-65; as custom, 79; moral, 17, 84-85, 87, 94. *See* Metalaw
League of Nations, 91
Lenin, V. I., 10
Lévi-Strauss, Claude, 34
Lévinas, Emmanuel, 22, 25, 35, 37, 41, 45, 60, 64, 69, 71
Lexis, 5
Liberalism, 21, 74
Listening, 22, 66, 71-72
Logic, 22, 24-25
Logos, 5
Ludendorff, Erich, 71
Lukács, Gÿorgy, 104
Lunacharsky, A. V., 10
Lyotard, Jean François: as Aristotelian, 26, 29; as Kantian, 70, 73, 88; and philosophy of the will, 89; on proper name, 102n8; role as writer, 3-9, 16-17, 54-55; article on Louis Marin, 15; *Discours, figure*, 55; *L'Economie libidinale*, 3-6, 89-90; *Just Gaming*, 6-7, 101-13, 118; *Instructions païennes*, 55-59; *The Postmodern Condition*, 104, 105, 110, 118; *Rudiments Païenes*, 15-16

Maiakovsky, V. V., 10
Majority, 99
Mallarmé, Stéphane, 12
Marin, Louis, 15
Marx, Karl, 20-21, 23, 25, 89
Marxism, 56, 74, 89, 104
Mastery, 6-7, 98, 112-13, 118
Mean, 26-27
Megaratics, 83
Message, 58

Meta-addressee, 57
Metalanguage, 28, 43, 58, 98-99
Metalaw, 52
Michelet, Jules, 13
Miltiades, 107
Mimèsis, 18, 19
Minority, 95-96, 99
Model, 17, 18, 22-23, 25, 27, 29, 30, 31
Modernity: addressee in, 10; author's role in, 9-11; and humor, 12; and justice, 29-30, 66; lack of criteria in, 15-16; as paganism, 16; in politics, 16n, 30; prescription in, 17, 29-30; and Romanticism, 11, 16n; untimeliness of, 13-14; will in, 18
Monism, 90, 96, 101
Montaigne, Michel Eyquem de, 8
Morality, 17, 18, 25-26, 30, 46, 81, 84, 87, 88, 91, 93, 94
Moro, Aldo, 70
Moses, 22, 54
Motif, 69
Moves, 54; invention of, 61-62, 100, 103
Multiplicity. *See* Language games, plurality of; Plurality
Murder, 63
Music, 34, 61; pop music, 12-13
Mythology, 38, 60; Greek, 16, 17, 39, 42, 107; Roman, 16

Nambikwara, 41
Name. *See* Denomination; Proper name
Narratee, privileging of, 33, 36, 41, 43
Narrative, 12, 17, 53, 60, 96; great, 59; popular, 32-35, 38, 39-40, 110-11, 118; and prescription, 99, 104, 108
Nature. *See* Suprasensible nature
Nazism, 74
Nietzsche, Friedrich, 14, 18, 44, 89, 113, 120n8; "Homer's Contest," 105-8
Nostalgia, 14

Obligation, 17, 35, 37, 38, 42, 45, 46, 60, 64, 65, 69-70, 72, 86, 88, 92, 97. *See also* Prescription
Obsession, 109
Oedipus, 42
Opinion, 27, 28, 29, 43, 57, 74, 77, 78, 95; in Aristotle, 75-76; in Kant, 79-83; maximization of, 78-79; 81; politics of, 75-76, 82, 88; public, 67-68, 70
Oracle, 36, 39, 42

Origin, lost, 20
Other, 22, 39, 60, 103, 105, 106, 107

Paganism: and Aristotle, 27-28, 29; and autonomy, 31; heteronomy of, 36; and justice, 19; as Kantian Idea, 58; and narrative, 110; and the people, 38; and plurality of language games, 61-62; and politics, 75; and postmodernity, 16n; and prescription, 16-18, 59; and science, 30-31; specificity of, 60-62; and time, 34; and "totality of reasonable beings," 76-77; and tradition, 33; will in, 18. *See also* Gods, pagan
Pagus, 38, 42
Paradox, 21, 82, 102
Paralogism, 80, 82
Paris Commune, 21
Parmenides, 54, 57, 62
Pascal, Blaise, 15, 18, 81
Passivity, 37-38
Pathos, 20
Pausanias, 107
Peithô, 4
People, the, 12-13
Periodization, 16n, 18
Persuasion, 4
Phantasm, 49
Phantasma, 75, 81
Philosopher-king, 20
Phronésis, 26, 95
Piety, 20
Plato, 4, 25, 27, 29, 30, 33, 35, 38, 57, 81; dialogue in, 56-57; on justice, 19-21, 22-23
Pléonexia, 97, 99
Plurality (multiplicity), 94-100, 102. *See also* Language games, plurality of
Politéa, 21
Politics, 16, 20, 36, 49, 55, 56, 64, 93; of capital, 90, 101-2; and knowledge, 28, 73-74; of Ideas, 95; of opinion, 75-76, 82, 88; and plurality, 94-100; of practical reason, 84-85; prescription in, 23; rational, 75, 77, 81-82, 89
Ponto, Jürgen, 68
Postmodernity, 16n
Postulates, 45-46, 47
Practical reason, 87-88, 92; politics of, 84-85; Practice, 18, 22, 28, 73
Pragmatics, of discourse, 31, 34, 35, 38, 41, 52, 54-56, 91, 93; of dreams, 110

Pragmatic triangle, 71
Prayer, 22, 23
Prescription: change of over time, 62-63; and denotation, 21-24, 44-45, 50-51, 59, 64, 69, 85, 86, 96; and dialectics, 27; domination by, 104-5; exceptions to, 63-64; in Judaism, 17, 37-39, 41-42, 63-64, 65-66; and justice, 25; in Kant, 85-86; as language game, 50; local, 57; and logic, 24-25; in modernity, 17, 29-30; and narrative, 99, 104, 108; in paganism, 16-18, 59; in politics, 23; relaying of, 31, 32, 35, 39, 110; singularity of, 51-52; and transcendence, 98; universal, 100. *See also* Obligation
Presentation, of the unpresentable, 105
Prolepsis, 112
Proper name, 32, 40, 51, 62, 120n
Propositions, 45
Proscription, 103, 104-5
Protagoras, 78, 95
Psychè, 23

Racine, Jean, 16
Reader, 4, 6, 8-11
Real, 23, 48-49, 50, 57, 58, 66, 76-77, 98. *See also* Content, Referent
Reason, 27, 46, 86; of history, 73, 74; political, 87-88; politics of, 82, 89. *See also* Practical reason
Rebellion, 66, 70, 76
Reception, 9
Red Army Fraction, 67, 107
Referent, 36, 41, 86, 98; privileging of, 21, 24, 33. *See also* Content, Real
Relaying, of prescriptions, 31, 32, 35, 39, 110
Religion, 18
Representation, 20, 75, 81
Request, 22, 23, 25
Rescher, Nicholas, 24
Rhythm, 34-35, 101, 118
Robespierre, Maximilien, 98
Romanticism: irony in, 12, 14; and modernity, 11-13, 16n
Rousseau, Jean-Jacques, 29, 30, 35
Ruse, 8, 16, 40, 41, 43, 61, 80-81

Satire, 60
Saussure, Ferdinand de, 50
"Savage" societies, 17
Schleyer, Hanns-Martin, 67, 70, 108

Schmidt, Helmut, 68
Searle, John R., 37
Secondary revision, in dreams, 113
Self, 113, 118
Self-management, 31
Semantikos, 22
Semiotics, 15, 89
Sender (speaker, utterer), 6, 23, 30, 31, 38-
    40, 63, 110; occulted, 71-72; privileging
    of, 36. *See also* Author, Subject of
    enunciation
Sensus communis, 14
Signified, 62
Simulacrum, 4
Skeptics, 74
Slogan, 55, 57, 58
So daß, 47
Social bond, 29, 30, 32, 71, 91, 93, 99
Society, 10, 20, 22-23, 25, 73, 82, 86; Idea
    of, 58, 85
Sophists, 5, 17, 25, 29, 64-65, 66, 73-74,
    75, 77, 78, 80, 82, 83, 95
Sophocles, 42
Speaker. *See* Sender
Speech, 50; compared to writing, 8
Sprachgesang, 34
Statements, 54, 110; classes of 22-23, 24
Stoics, 48-49
Strategy, 17, 27, 55
Struggle, 104, 105-6
Subject of the enunciation, 30, 31, 33, 36-37
Sublation, 53
Suprasensible nature, 75, 76, 82, 85
Synthesis, 79, 90
System, 104

Talmud, 39, 41
Taste, 9, 11, 12, 16*n*
Tekhnè, 28, 78
Teleology, 47, 84, 88, 96
Terror, 63, 67-68, 71, 92, 99-100, 102, 107-
    8; "rationalist," 74
Time, 34, 83
Totalitarianism, 18, 96, 103
Totality (unity), 58, 86, 87-88, 93, 95, 97;
    absence of, 94
"Totality of reasonable beings," 46, 75, 76-
    77, 83, 85, 91, 93
Tradition, 33, 34

Transcendence, 60, 69-70, 71, 98, 113
Transference, 113
Translation, 53
Truth, 6, 20, 22, 23-24, 27, 28, 29, 31, 38,
    43, 57, 60, 62, 75, 97, 98, 99
"Two Discourses" (*Dissoi Logoi*), 80

Ulysses, 39-40
Unconscious, 109-12
Understanding, 26, 27, 41, 42, 90, 95
Unity. *See* Totality
Universality, 5, 11, 47, 56, 57, 77, 94, 98,
    103
Untimeliness, 13-14
Urteil, 115, 116-17
Use-value, 104
Utterance. *See* Enunciation
Utterer. *See* Sender

Vanguard, artistic, 10
Velocity, 90, 101-2
Verisimilitude, 74, 75-76, 78
Verkehr, 119
Vernant, Jean-Pierre, 16
Verneinung, 48
Vernichthungskampf, 106-7
Vernunft, 27
Verstand, 27
Vietnam, 69
Violence, 4, 63, 67, 100, 102, 103, 108
Virtù, 18
Virtue, 26
Volo, 29-30

War, 67, 71, 99, 108
Weber, Max, 27
Wettkampf, 106
Will, 18, 29-31, 35, 47, 61, 74, 84, 87, 91;
    philosophy of, 89-90, 96, 101-2
Will to power, 17
Witz (joke), 103, 105, 113, 117
Wright, G. H. von, 24
Writer. *See* Author, Sender
Writing: audience for, 8-11; author's role,
    3-9; effects on reader, 4; experimenta-
    tion in, 9-10; irresponsibility of, 8. *See
    also* Discourse; Language games

Zwangshandlungen, 109

JEAN-FRANÇOIS LYOTARD (1925–1998) was one of the principal French philosophers and intellectuals of the twentieth century. His works include *The Postmodern Condition*, *Postmodern Fables*, and *Signed, Malraux*, all published by the University of Minnesota Press.

JEAN-LOUP THÉBAUD was editor of *L'esprit*.

WLAD GODZICH is professor of comparative literature at the University of Geneva.

SAMUEL WEBER is professor of English and comparative literature at the University of California, Los Angeles.